Rosie
THE
Riveter

Front cover: "Rosie" by Norman Rockwell. This painting appeared on the cover of the Saturday Evening Post *on May 29, 1943. Mr. Rockwell discussed a mistake he had made in a newspaper article published that week: "I made a mistake in detail that people will be calling me down for. The cover shows Rosie with goggles on* and *an isinglass protective shield. I don't think riveters use both. It was silly of me."*

Rosie
THE
Riveter

Women Working
on the Home Front
in World War II

★

Penny Colman

ILLUSTRATED WITH PHOTOGRAPHS

Crown Publishers, Inc.   New York

To all the women who have been pioneers in the workplace

Poem on page 19 from *On Wings to War: Teresa James, Aviator* by Jan Churchill, Sunflower University Press, 1992. Reprinted by permission of the author.

Lyrics from "Rosie the Riveter" on pages 15–16 copyright © 1942 (renewed 1969) John J. Loeb Company and Music Sales Corporation. Exclusive licensee for John J. Loeb Company: Fred Ahlert Music Corporation. International copyright secured. All rights reserved.

Published by Crown Publishers, Inc., a Random House company, 201 East 50th Street, New York, New York 10022

CROWN is a trademark of Crown Publishers, Inc.

http://www.randomhouse.com/

Printed in the United States of America

Photo credits appear on page 114.

Library of Congress Cataloging-in-Publication Data
Colman, Penny.
Rosie the riveter: women working on the home front in World War II / by Penny Colman.
p.   cm.
Includes bibliographical references and index.
1. Women—Employment—United States—History—20th century—Juvenile literature. 2. World War, 1939–1945—Women—United States—Juvenile Literature. [1. Women—Employment—History. 2. World War, 1939–1945—United States.] I. Title.
HD6095.C64   1995
331.4'0973'09044—dc20   94-3614
ISBN 0-517-59790-X (trade)
ISBN 0-517-59791-8 (lib. bdg.)
ISBN 0-517-88567-0 (pbk.)

10 9 8 7 6 5 4 3 2

CONTENTS

ONE

War!
"How are things going to change?"

The summer between second and third grade, Dot Chastney had her first inkling that things weren't quite right in the world. It was 1939 and Annie Ashworth, the woman who lived across the street from Dot in Hasbrouck Heights, New Jersey, had gone to Europe on a vacation. "Before she left, she told my mother that she would bring her some linen cloth from Ireland. She knew that my mother loved to sew," Dot remembers. Ireland was just one of the many countries in Europe that Annie Ashworth was going to visit. She had been planning and saving for her trip for years. "She was so excited. It was a dream trip of a lifetime for her," says Dot.

Annie Ashworth was supposed to return in August. But by the middle of August, Dot knew something was wrong. "In those days parents didn't talk about a whole lot of things in front of their children. But I overheard my parents talking about the trouble that Annie Ashworth was having getting home from Europe. I couldn't quite figure out what was going on, but I knew there was a problem," says Dot.

The problem was Adolf Hitler and the German army.

Head of the National Socialist (Nazi) party, Hitler had ruled Germany since 1933. He told the German people that he would build Germany into a mighty empire. He told his soldiers, "Close your eyes to pity! Act brutally!" In March 1938, Hitler's troops crossed the Austrian border and took over Austria. In September

Dot Chastney in third grade.

1938 they took over Sudetenland, a part of Czechoslovakia. By March 1939, they had taken over the rest of Czechoslovakia. "Conquest is not only a right but a duty," Hitler said.

Some people spoke out against Hitler. But they weren't strong enough to stop him. Within Germany, Hitler's secret police, known as the Gestapo, destroyed anyone who opposed him. In

In front of the White House, 1941: An American soldier grabs a sign from an isolationist who is picketing against entering the war.

1933 the first concentration camp was built at Dachau, Germany. Other concentration camps were built as Hitler escalated his efforts to eliminate anyone he considered undesirable. Gypsies were sent to concentration camps to die. So were communists, gay men and lesbians, people with mental or physical disabilities, and millions and millions of Jews.

Outside of Germany the leaders of France and Great Britain thought they could appease Hitler by letting him take some territory, hoping that would satisfy him. Leaders of other countries, such as Benito Mussolini, the dictator of Italy, signed treaties of friendship with Hitler. So did the military leaders of Japan. On August 24, 1939, while Annie Ashworth was in Europe, Russia signed a nonaggression treaty with Germany that shocked the world. The two countries agreed to "refrain from every act of force, every aggressive action, and every attack against one another."

Now that Hitler knew Russia wasn't a threat, he made his move.

At dawn on September 1, 1939, German troops, tanks, and aircraft attacked Poland, the country that lay between Russia and Germany. Great Britain and France warned Hitler that they would go to war if he didn't withdraw his troops. Hitler ignored them. And so on September 3, Great Britain and France declared war on Germany, officially starting World War II.

Dot was never quite sure how Annie Ashworth got out of Europe. But she did, sometime in September after school had started. "I remember that she came over and sat on our front porch with my mother. She didn't say much when I was around, just that she had managed to get to England and then to Canada. From there she took a train home and had to sit up all night," says Dot. Although Dot worried how she would have gotten home if

If we permit our country to become involved in the wars now raging in Europe, Asia and Africa, we face disastrous sacrifices — human, social and material. We risk the liberties of the United States in a conflict from which no nation can emerge truly victorious. Let us spare America from such an act of national folly.

AMERICA FIRST COMMITTEE
141 West Jackson Blvd.   Chicago, Illinois

she had been Annie Ashworth, she knew that the fighting was far away from America.

Americans were determined to stay out of the fighting. World War I had left most Americans disillusioned about war. After all, they had fought that war believing that it was the "war to end all wars," but now another war was raging. Americans had also been disillusioned when a Senate investigation revealed that many American businessmen had made huge sums of money out of World War I. People called them "merchants of death."

In addition, the United States was still recovering from the Great Depression, which had left millions of Americans struggling to find jobs, food, and housing. Dot's parents had gotten married four months before the stock market crashed in October 1929, the event that marked the beginning of the Great Depression. She remembers her mother saying, "There were times during the depression when we didn't know what to use for money. But everybody was in the same boat."

Although most Americans didn't want to get involved in the war, they paid attention to what was happening. Every night Dot and her family ate dinner in the kitchen with the little radio on, listening to Edward R. Murrow, an American news reporter, broadcasting from London. "His voice coming through the static was incredible. We could really hear the bombs whistling in the background," says Dot. She also saw newsreels about the war at movie theaters and saw war photographs in magazines such as *Life.* Everyday her father brought home several newspapers. War news was everywhere. And it wasn't good.

In 1940, Hitler added more countries to his conquered list— Norway, Denmark, Luxembourg, Belgium, the Netherlands, and France. German bombers blasted Britain, and German submarines

sank huge numbers of ships. Italy invaded more countries. So did Japan. Then, on June 22, 1941, in a stunning turnaround, Germany violated its nonaggression agreement and invaded Russia.

As the war spread, the United States responded in various ways. In 1940, Congress voted to spend more money for national defense. It also passed the Selective Training and Service Act, which set up a system for drafting men into the armed forces. In March 1941, Congress passed the Lend-Lease Act, which gave the president authority to send weapons, food, and equipment to Great Britain. But still Americans were determined to stay out of the fighting.

May 29, 1941: A rally held by the America First Committee fills Madison Square Garden in New York City. With 800,000 members, the America First Committee was a political group that aggressively opposed America's involvement in the war. Famous aviator Charles Lindbergh was one of their outspoken leaders. His speeches were heard around the country by audiences like the one seen here.

December 8, 1941: A crowd at City Hall in New York listens as President Roosevelt asks Congress to declare war on Japan.

Then on December 7, 1941, a Sunday, 360 Japanese dive bombers, torpedo planes, and fighters attacked the U.S. naval base at Pearl Harbor. Caught by surprise, the U.S. fleet was devastated—2,403 Americans died, five battleships sank, other ships were severely damaged, and 200 planes were destroyed.

"Where is Pearl Harbor?" Dot asked when she first heard the news. "When my parents said, 'Hawaii,' I knew where that was."

Dot and her parents listened to the radio all day long. "It was so scary. Over and over I kept wondering, 'How are things going to change?'"

The next day, Monday, Dot's teacher brought a radio to class to listen to President Franklin Delano Roosevelt (FDR, as most people called him) speak to Congress. He began with the words "Yesterday, December 7, 1941, a date which will live in infamy . . ." and ended with the words, "I ask that the Congress declare that since the unprovoked and dastardly attack by Japan on Sunday, December 7, a state of war has existed between the United States and the Japanese Empire."

"We were very quiet," Dot remembers.

Congress voted to declare war on Japan. Several days later Germany and Italy declared war on the United States, and the United States declared war on Germany and Italy. The United States, Great Britain, France, Russia, and forty-five other countries that joined with them became known as the Allies. Germany, Japan, Italy, and three other countries became known as the Axis.

Now that America was involved in the fighting, almost everything in the United States began to change—some things immediately, other things gradually. Some things changed forever, other things changed just for the duration of the war. But almost everything changed.

TWO

The Home Front
"The exit of life-as-usual"

One change that Dot soon noticed was that many everyday items were in short supply: sugar, rubber, gasoline, heating oil, and coffee, among other things. And no new bicycles were made for almost five years. "My father had promised me that I could get a large two-wheel bicycle. When they stopped making them, I was heartbroken," Dot recalls. "When the war ended, I finally got a two-wheeler, but by then I was in the eighth grade!"

Bicycles were on the list of "casualties among civilian finished goods and staples" published in *Business Week* magazine four months after Pearl Harbor. According to *Business Week*, the list of items that would be no longer manufactured foretold "the rapidly approaching exit of life-as-usual" and included electrical appliances such as toasters and waffle irons; flashlights and batteries; fasteners such as zippers and snaps; tea; toys and games; vacuum cleaners; and vending machines. In addition, the supply of gasoline was reduced by 20 percent on the East Coast. Chicle, the main ingredient in bubble gum, was no longer available and so a synthetic rubber was used to make Dot's favorite bubble gum, Fleer's Double Bubble. "It had a grainy texture and my tongue would go right through it when I tried to blow a bubble."

There were several reasons for the shortages. American ships that ordinarily brought goods such as coffee beans from South America were now carrying troops. America's supply of rubber was cut off as Japan conquered countries in Southeast Asia. Silk produced in Japan was no longer available. In addition, metals—steel, zinc, nickel, tin—that had been used to make bicycles, flashlights, and vending machines were now needed to make tanks and armaments. Alcohol was needed to make explosives. Americans got used to seeing signs and posters with the words "Use it up/Wear it out/Make it do/Or do without."

To keep prices from soaring because of the shortages, FDR set up the Office of Price Administration and Civilian Supply Management (soon simply called Office of Price Administration or OPA). The OPA set up a system of rationing, or controlling the amount of certain items that people could buy. During the war, the OPA rationed twenty essential items, including rubber, shoes, and butter. In May 1942 sugar was rationed. Nationwide rationing of gasoline began in September. In November coffee was added to the list of rationed items. For the duration, citizens were issued war

Waiting in line at a shoe rationing board in New Orleans. Hundreds of rationing boards were set up by the Office of Price Administration (OPA) soon after America's entry into the war.

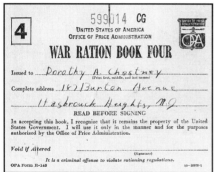

Dot's ration book, identical to those the OPA issued to every man, woman, and child in the United States.

ration books with pages of stamps that determined how many rationed items they could buy. Having money to buy a rationed item wasn't enough. Shoppers also had to have the right amount in ration stamps. Shoppers frequently had to stand in line to buy rationed items. But not Dot's mother: "My mother always said that if she had to stand in line, we didn't need it. So we learned to do without a lot," Dot remembers.

Everywhere Americans looked, they were reminded of rationing. Lunchboxes were made of fiberboard and stamped with the information that "Customary use of metal for your lunch kit has been forbidden . . . as steel is needed for war materials. This 'Victory Kit' is provided to take the place of your metal kit. Made of durable fiberboard, it is sturdily constructed to give you good service. . . . Because of the nature of the material, this kit should not be left or stored in damp or wet locations."

Charlcia Neuman, who worked long hours at an airplane factory, relied on her daughter to do the shopping and to deal with the complexities of rationing. "I had a daughter who was very capable. She took the ration books and she figured that all out. She was in junior high school at the time. It helped make her a stronger person, I'm sure."

Americans were also asked to save and salvage scrap metal, newspapers, waste fat, aluminum and tin cans, rubber, nylon and silk stockings. One pound of waste fat—bacon grease, meat drippings, frying fat—contained enough glycerin to manufacture a pound of black powder that could be used in bullets. Nylon and silk stockings were made into parachutes and towropes for glider planes. One old shovel contained enough iron to make four hand grenades. One 2,000-pound bomb could be made from 12,000 razor blades.

Massive drives were sponsored by the War Production Board

(WPB). Created by FDR in January 1942, the WPB had the power to decide which scarce material went to which factory and how many civilian goods, such as refrigerators, were going to be made during the war, if any were to be made at all. There were official fat-collecting stations, scrap-metal drives, newspaper drives, and a national aluminum drive. Abandoned trolley tracks were dug up and donated to the war effort. The city of Griffin, Georgia, donated antique fire engines. Students at the City College of New York collected the tinfoil wrappers from sticks of chewing gum and cigarette packages. In June 1942 a nationwide rubber drive was held. FDR asked people to collect "old tires, old rubber raincoats, old garden hoses, bathing caps, gloves—whatever you have that is made of rubber."

Dot and her best friend Madeline collected newspapers and

The War Production Board (WPB) used photographs like this one to encourage women to contribute time to the war effort. The original caption read: "STOCKINGS FOR VICTORY New York . . . Mrs. Henry C. McDuff of New York is snowed under with silk and nylon stockings. More than a mile of the valuable silk and nylon stockings have been collected in a week by members of the New York Vassar Club. There are many ways the material can be put to war use."

Volunteer civilian plane spotters in Monroe, North Carolina.

took them to a collection center. "I hated it. It was so boring. We took my brother's little red wagon and went around to the neighbors. My mother made me do it because she thought it would teach me to be responsible." Dot and Madeline also looked out for spies, as did many Americans, because the government frequently sent out warnings. "Whenever we saw someone suspicious-looking, someone who wouldn't look us in the eye or gave us a furtive look or walked funny, we would say, 'Maybe they're a spy.'"

The government also asked Americans to plant victory gardens. At one point there were nearly twenty million victory gardens in America that were producing a third of all the vegetables grown in the country. Dot's family had one. "We grew lettuce, soybeans, tomatoes, and radishes. My father did the digging. My job was to pull the Japanese beetles off the soybean plants and put them in a bottle of kerosene. I thought it was kind of fun," Dot remembers.

One year Dot's father "shocked all the neighbors" when he had a truckload of cow manure dumped in their driveway. "My father loaded it in his wheelbarrow and shoveled it all around the victory garden. He insisted that it was absolutely the best thing for the garden. I can still remember the smell," Dot says.

To help pay for the staggering costs of the war, the government asked Americans to buy war bonds for $18.75 each. In ten years, each bond would be worth $25. Americans could also buy stamps for ten cents or more and paste them into a book until they added up to $18.75. During the war, eight huge war-bond drives were held. Advertisements for bonds appeared everywhere—on billboards and the sides of railroad cars. Hundreds of posters advertised war bonds. Clowns at the Barnum and Bailey Circus, movie stars, comedians, and politicians pushed war bonds. There were bond booths at movie theaters and grocery stores. People regularly used part of each paycheck to buy bonds. So did Dot.

Children in violin class at the National Institute of Music and Arts in Bremerton, Washington, pose in the shape of a "V for Victory" while holding up their bonds and savings stamps. The letter V first began appearing on walls in German-occupied Belgium. In French the V stands for victoire *(victory), and in Flemish the V stands for* vrigheid *(freedom). As Germany conquered more countries, the use of the V spread as a protest sign. The use of the V for victory eventually spread to the United States.*

"Once a week I would bring in ten or twenty-five cents to school and buy war-bond savings stamps and paste them in little booklets. Practically every kid in my class did that."

The war transformed every aspect of life on the home front. Radio broadcasts were dominated by war news. According to Dot, "I used to ask my father all the time, 'What do the men on the news talk about when there is no war?'"

In addition to war news, Americans listened to a radio series called *This Is War*. One radio program in the series was written by the famous poet Stephen Vincent Benét and included a line about soldiers guaranteed to inspire home front patriotism: "They're going to die in the jungles for the shape of a Virginia field and the crossroads store back home—they're going to die in the cold, for the clear air of Montana and the smell of a New York street."

Movies had war themes. *Thirty Seconds Over Tokyo* was the true story of a daredevil raid on Tokyo in 1942. Popular songs, often written at the request of the government, promoted everything from salvage drives and war bonds to victory gardens and civil defense. Catchy tunes were written with titles such as "Get Out and Dig, Dig, Dig (Your Victory Garden)," "Junk Ain't Junk No More (Save and Salvage)," "Get Aboard the Bond Wagon," "Shhh! It's a Military Secret," "When the Air Raid Siren Sounds," and "Remember Pearl Harbor." Kate Smith's rousing rendition of Irving Berlin's song "God Bless America" became an unofficial national anthem.

The war and appeals to patriotism permeated everything on the home front. "Life was absolutely consumed by the war," Dot remembers. And if people forgot, there was always someone around to remind them by repeating the common saying "Don't you know there's a war on?"

One of Dot's savings stamps.

THREE

Extraordinary Opportunities for Women
"Rosie the Riveter"

Although Dot was not old enough to be affected, one of the most dramatic changes during World War II was the extraordinary job opportunities for women. As the armed forces filled its ranks with *manpower*, industry filled its jobs with *womanpower*. For the duration of the war, the U.S. government and industry wooed American women to work in the war effort on the home front. The title of a song, "Rosie the Riveter," quickly became the catchphrase that represented all women war workers. Written by Redd Evans and John Jacob Loeb in 1942, "Rosie the Riveter" was first released in February 1943. The upbeat song was heard on the radio, on records, and in coin-operated machines located in restaurants and bus and train stations that played three-minute versions of songs called "soundies." According to Janet Loeb, the widow of John Jacob Loeb, the title was not based on a real person but was selected because of its alliteration. During the war the song was featured in two movies: *Follow the Band* in 1943 and *Rosie the Riveter* in 1944. Originally sung by The Four Vagabonds, a group of male singers, the song began with these lyrics:

> *While other girls attend a favorite cocktail bar,*
> *Sipping dry martinis, munching caviar;*
> *There's a girl who's really putting them to shame—*
> *Rosie is her name.*

This image of a woman war worker appeared on the cover of the Saturday Evening Post *on May 29, 1943. Painted by Norman Rockwell, the woman worker has a big, muscular body and a cute, saucy face and pose. Her rivet gun is resting across her lap and the name Rosie is painted on her lunchbox. The model for the cover was Mary Doyle, a nineteen-year-old telephone operator in Arlington, Vermont.*

All the day long, whether rain or shine,
She's part of the assembly line,
She's making history working for victory,
Rosie, Rosie, Rosie, Rosie, Rosie, Rosie the riveter.

During World War II, more than six million women joined the workforce. In August 1943, *Newsweek* magazine reported: "They [women] are in the shipyards, lumber mills, steel mills, foundries. They are welders, electricians, mechanics, and even boilermakers. They operate streetcars, buses, cranes, and tractors. Women engineers are working in the drafting rooms and women

Inspecting the end of a 40mm artillery cartridge case at Frankford Arsenal (opposite left). Scrubbing the interior of a Pennsylvania Railroad coach (opposite right). Operating a trolley car in Brooklyn, New York (this page).

physicists and chemists in the great industrial laboratories." More than two million women joined the war effort as clerical workers, nearly one million of whom were hired by the federal government. Women also became police officers, taxicab drivers, lawyers, statisticians, journalists, and members of symphony orchestras as men left for the armed forces. Women ran farms, planted crops, tended animals, and harvested tons of vegetables, fruits, and grains.

Transporting bales of hay on a Midwestern farm.

In addition, three million women served as Red Cross volunteers. Millions of women worked for the Civilian Defense as air-raid wardens, fire watchers, messengers, drivers, auxiliary police. They also devoted hours to scanning the sky with binoculars, looking out for enemy planes. Thousands of women joined the military, including Teresa D. James, a pilot for the Women's Air Force Service Pilots (WASP). On September 22, 1944, Teresa James flew the ten-thousandth P-47 Thunderbolt fighter plane that was produced at the Republic Aviation factory in Farmingdale, New York, to the Newark Army Base in Newark, New Jersey.

Named *Ten Grand*, the ten-thousandth plane had been made by the Racers, as the workers at Republic were called. Half of the Racers were women. The year before she flew *Ten Grand*, James had written a poem that included these lines:

> *We knew from the first that we were resented,*
> *By the continued aloofness which the men presented . . .*
> *It's tough, we know, but we are game,*
> *We'll fight no end to make a name.*
> *Remarks and opinions just egg us on*
> *To win a place where we rightfully belong.*

By the time World War II ended, America's wartime production record included 296,429 airplanes; 102,351 tanks and self-propelled guns; 372,431 artillery pieces; 47 million tons of artillery ammunition; 87,620 warships; and 44 billion rounds of small-arms ammunition. *Time* magazine called America's wartime production a miracle.

The "miracle" would not have happened without Rosie the

At Boeing. The woman on the left works as a riveter while the woman on the right works as a bucker. The riveter inserts the rivet (a bolt with a head at one end) into a hole that has been drilled or punched into the metal. The bucker uses a metal bar called a bucking bar to shape the other end of the rivet into a second head that holds the metal together.

Riveter, who in real life was a woman like JoAnn Hudlicky, who recalled how she became a crane operator. "I saw the cranes, and so I grabbed my boss one day, and I said, 'How do you get a job running a crane?' And he said, 'Do you think you can do that?' And I said, 'Well, I don't know why I can't, other people are doing it.' . . . I put everything into it I could, 'cause I really wanted to do it." Or like another woman who recalled her first day on the job as a welder in a shipyard. She was eighteen years old. "Well, I got in the little compartment, see, it was either the officers' head or the shower, I forget which, and I got in there and so I got my [protective] hood down. I got the stinger out and I started to run a weld up this bulkhead. So I took the [hood] off and [the weld] had all run down and it looked terrible. I didn't know what to do. I just put my hood down and sat there and cried. I said, 'I'm too young. I'm too little to do this job.' And so I sat there about fifteen or twenty minutes and said, 'Well, I'm going to try it anyway.' So I worked my way up, and lo and behold, I worked my way up to the top and it got better and better all along."

Or like Rose Bonavita and Jennie Fiorito, who drove a record 3,345 rivets into the wing of a Grumman Avenger torpedo bomber on June 8, 1943, while working the midnight to 6:00 A.M. shift. Bonavita and Fiorito worked for Eastern Aircraft in Tarrytown, New York. The newspaper in Bonavita's home town, Peekskill, New York, dubbed her "Peekskill's Rosie." Although the song "Rosie the Riveter" was released five months before Bonavita set the record, some writers have since claimed that Rosie the Riveter was based on Rose Bonavita. Years after the war, Bonavita herself was quoted as saying, "I wasn't *the* 'Rosie the Riveter' and I never claimed to be."

When the war ended in 1945, so did the extraordinary job opportunities for women. Rosie the Riveter disappeared as quickly as she had been created. According to William Mulcahy, who supervised women war workers who assembled sensitive electronic parts, "Unfortunately, when the war ended, despite the skill and patriotism the women had displayed, we were forced to lay them off. I will never forget the day after the war ended. We met the girls at the door, and they were lined up all the way down Market Street [in Camden, New Jersey] to the old movie theater about eight blocks away, and we handed them a slip to go over to personnel and get their severance pay. We didn't even allow them in the building, all these women with whom I had become so

close, who had worked seven days a week for years and had been commended so many times by the navy for the work they were doing."

Although America no longer needed women workers, the story of their wartime achievements and contributions is found in the words and writings of women and men who lived during World War II; in employment records and statistics; magazine and newspaper articles; radio programs; and thousands of posters, pamphlets, and photographs. This is an amazing story about a time when stereotypes about men's work and women's work were suspended. When traditional barriers that had blocked women workers were lowered. And when women had a chance to prove what they could do.

FOUR

Getting Ready for War
"The great arsenal for democracy"

The story of women workers in World War II begins with the story of America's extraordinary industrial mobilization. According to Donald Nelson, head of the War Production Board, "This is the record: For nine years before Pearl Harbor, Germany, Italy, and Japan prepared intensively for war, while as late as 1940 the war production of peaceful America was virtually nothing. Yet two years later the output of our war factories equaled that of the three Axis nations combined."

Anticipating America's involvement in the war, FDR called in May 1940 for an increase in production of matériel (equipment, apparatus, and supplies)—more than a year and a half before Pearl Harbor. "I believe that this nation should plan at this time a

The New York World-Telegram *from May 16, 1940. This copy belonged to Dot Chastney's father.*

program that would provide us with fifty thousand military and naval planes," he said in a speech to Congress. In December, FDR announced that the United States "must be the great arsenal for democracy."

Throughout 1940, U.S. industry increased its production of war matériel. As new jobs were created, the number of unemployed people dropped, finally signaling the end of the Great Depression. Men were the first people hired, but as the need for workers increased, employers slowly began hiring women. In early 1941, Vultee Aircraft Company in Los Angeles, California, hired twenty-five women. In East Longmeadow, Massachusetts, the Springfield Armory hired fourteen women.

Still, many employers refused to hire women. According to the men in charge, women did not have the physical strength, mechanical ability, and emotional stability to do high-paying, skilled factory jobs. In addition, employers said, the presence of women would distract men.

Discrimination in the workplace was nothing new for women. It had existed throughout American history. With few exceptions, women had been barred from jobs or professions that paid well or had status.

The barriers against women workers had been heightened by the Great Depression, when jobs were very scarce. Married women bore the brunt of the prejudice because many people thought that one salary should be enough to support any family. Laws were passed that prohibited married women from getting jobs in local government. During the 1930–31 school year, a survey of fifteen hundred school districts reported that 77 percent of the districts refused to hire married women and 63 percent of them fired women teachers if they married. In 1936, 82 percent

THE PHILADELPHIA GAS WORKS COMPANY

1800 NORTH NINTH STREET

PHILADELPHIA

February 24, 1942

Miss Mary Anderson,
Director, Women's Bureau,
U. S. Department of Labor,
Washington, D. C.

Dear Miss Anderson:

For several years this Company has operated
under a rule, known to all of its women employees, re-
quiring women employees who marry to sever their employment with the Company. Of the women employees
who have married and thus lost their employment with
this Company, most of those who have desired to continue working have been placed by us in employment
with other organizations.

The wartime situation, however, has caused us
to temporarily suspend our rule concerning married
women so that they will be permitted to remain for the
duration of the emergency, after which time they will
be given notice of severance, the length of the notice
varying according to the length of service credit.

Very truly yours,

THE PHILADELPHIA GAS WORKS COMPANY

C. G. Simpson,
Manager, Personnel Department

CGS:JWH

LET *Gas* DO THE 4 BIG JOBS—Cooking · Refrigeration · Water Heating · House Heating

This letter from the director of personnel at the Philadelphia Gas Works Company notified the director of the Women's Bureau of the U.S. Department of Labor of a change in policy regarding the status of married women employees for the duration of the war.

of all Americans said that wives should not work if their husbands had a job. In 1939, 84 percent of insurance companies and 65 percent of banks put limits on married women working.

But in early 1941, anticipating the need to hire at least some women workers to fill the increasing number of defense jobs, the U.S. government made efforts to encourage the employment of women. A federal agency produced a ten-minute film, "Women in Defense." It was written by FDR's wife, Eleanor Roosevelt, and narrated by a popular actress, Katharine Hepburn. The film showed women in a variety of roles—including a scientist, a factory worker, and a Red Cross volunteer. "This woman is a modern pioneer" was one of the lines that Hepburn repeated many times in the film.

Several federal officials spoke out and urged defense industries to use women. Mary Anderson, head of the Women's Bureau of the Department of Labor, announced that there were nearly two million women available to work in defense industries. She worked at establishing job-training programs for women. Through the National Youth Administration (NYA), a program set up during the Great Depression to help unemployed youth, twenty thousand girls were learning such skills as welding and radio repair. Mary McLeod Bethune, director of the Division of Negro Affairs of the NYA, made sure black girls were included, a significant accomplishment since segregation was still legal in the United States.

The situation for black people in America was terrible. Three out of four black people lived in the South and struggled to survive as tenant farmers. Southern states had laws, known as Jim Crow laws, that forced black people to go to separate schools, ride in the back of streetcars and buses, live in separate neighborhoods, drink from separate water fountains, and stay out of "whites only" parks. Literacy tests and poll taxes were used to prevent black people from voting. Black people were beaten and lynched by groups of white people who joined secret organizations to maintain segregation.

Things were only a little better in the North. Although there were no laws that made segregation the official policy, white people held all the power and most black people lived apart in old, rundown neighborhoods with poor schools. There were few good job opportunities, and there was a great deal of on-the-job discrimination.

As America geared up for war, it became clear that black Americans were going to be needed in the military and in defense jobs. However, black soldiers were assigned to segregated units and black workers were often kept out of defense jobs. So many black Americans rallied together to insist that they be treated on an equal basis with white people. A widely circulated black newspaper announced a "Double V" campaign: one *V* for victory overseas against dictators, the other *V* for victory on the home

Picketers rally for defense jobs outside the Glenn Martin plant. While black men were drafted into the armed forces, they and black women were discriminated against for war jobs. And although black men were drafted, the armed forces remained segregated until 1948.

front against discrimination. At a 1940 civil rights convention in Chicago, a black woman delegate said, "We ought to throw fifty thousand Negroes around the White House, bring them from all over the country, in jalopies, in trains, and any way they can get there . . . until we get some action from the White House."

In January 1941 that's exactly what labor organizer A. Philip Randolph and a coalition of black leaders threatened to do: lead a march on Washington of fifty thousand black protesters. Hoping to get Randolph to call off the march, FDR met with him. But Randolph refused. Finally FDR agreed to issue an executive order banning discrimination. It said in part: "It is the policy of the United States to encourage full participation in the national defense program by all citizens of the United States, regardless of race, creed, color, or national origin." FDR also set up the Fair Employment Practices Commission (FEPC) to implement Executive Order 8802. Randolph agreed to call off the march on Washington.

While Executive Order 8802 and the FEPC were important achievements, discrimination continued, especially against women of color, who had to deal with both racism and sexism. Nevertheless, many African-American, Mexican-American, and Native American women made some wartime gains.

Eight hundred Native American women joined the military. Another twelve thousand Indian women left their reservations to work in war jobs. On the Menominee reservation in Wisconsin, Indian women began working in lumber mills. In Everett, Washington, Harriette Shelton Williams, daughter of the chief of the Snohomish Indians, worked at Boeing Aircraft Corporation. Also a poet, author, and interpreter of Indian dances and legends, she was known as Princess Hiahl-tsa, meaning Princess Shining

This picture of Harriette Shelton Williams appeared in the Boeing News *Bellingham/Everett edition, May 26, 1944. The original caption read: "She isn't dressed this way every day on her Boeing job, but fellow-workers say there's no mistaking the royal bearing of Princess Hiahl-tsa even when she wears work-a-day garb."*

Feather. Some Chinese and Filipina women got defense jobs. Because of the wartime need for their labor, a group of Mexican-American women who had been working for very low wages at the California Sanitary Canning Company were able to organize and win higher wages. Other Mexican-American women found jobs in shipyards and aircraft factories.

Large numbers of black women, who had been stuck in low-paying dead-end jobs as domestic servants and farm workers, got

Women engine cleaners working for the Pennsylvania Railroad in 1943.

war-related jobs—although usually they were the dirtiest, hardest, and most dangerous jobs. Large numbers of black women worked in munitions factories handling explosives. They were hired by the Pennsylvania Railroad in Baltimore as water and fire tenders to keep up the fire and steam in the locomotives. The meat-packing industry in Detroit hired black women for jobs that other workers refused to do. When no one else would do the job, the city of Baltimore finally hired black women as city street cleaners.

Some black women also worked as welders and riveters. Sybil Lewis got a job at Lockheed Aircraft in Los Angeles. After taking a short training course, Lewis was put to work riveting small airplane parts, mainly gasoline tanks. She later described her work. "The women worked in pairs. I was the riveter, and this big strong white girl from a cotton farm in Arkansas worked as the bucker. Bucking was harder than shooting rivets. It required more muscle. Riveting required more skill."

Although they were hired last after white women and black men, black women persevered and got higher-paying jobs than the ones they had before the war. According to Fanny Christina "Tina" Hill, who got a job at North American Aircraft in Los Angeles, "The war made me live better, it really did. My sister always said that Hitler was the one that got us out of the white folks' kitchen." For Japanese-American women, however, the door of opportunity slammed shut when FDR issued Executive Order 9066, which was an unprecedented violation of the civil rights of American citizens. By order of the president and with congressional support, 110,000 Japanese Americans from the West Coast were forced to give up their homes and businesses and confined in camps that were surrounded by barbed wire and guarded by armed soldiers.

FDR also used his power as president to set up agencies to prepare America for war. In April 1941 he had established the Office of Price Administration and Civilian Supply Management to keep prices at a stable level. In May he established the Office of Civilian Defense (OCD).

Headed by New York City Mayor Fiorello La Guardia, the OCD set up a wide range of programs for people who wanted to defend the home front. There were programs to cover every

Women welders at the Landers, Frary, and Clark plant in New Britain, Connecticut.

conceivable concern that civilians might have, including air-raid drills, first-aid instruction, and fire fighting. Although enthusiasm for the OCD lessened as it became clear that America was safe from enemy attack, at its height in mid-1943 the OCD had more than ten million volunteers. Barbara

Mortensen spent hours in her lookout tower in White Mountain National Forest in New Hampshire as an aircraft spotter. Twelve women students at the American University, in Washington, D.C., formed one of the first Civilian Defense Fire Guard brigades and prepared themselves to fight any firebombs that the enemy might drop on the university. Women skiers joined the Utah Council of Defense and performed mapping, first-aid, and ski patrol duties. Women made blackout curtains to use

The Office of Civilian Defense (OCD) convinced families to turn their houses into "Victory homes." This image of two children was accompanied by the following: "THIS HOME SALVAGES ESSENTIAL MATERIALS. Sally cuts out the bottoms while Dave flattens out tin cans to turn over to salvage collectors. Cans must be rustless and stripped of paper to be suitable for 'de-tinning,' which helps keep supplies of the metal available for essential civilian as well as military uses."

The OCD often provided instructions, such as: "BLACKING OUT WINDOWS WITH IMPROVISED BLACKOUT SHADES. Ordinary blankets, taken from the bed if you have no spares, make fairly good blackout window shades in a pinch. Mrs. R. A. Wetzler of the American Women's Volunteer Service, is assisting Mrs. Galef in blacking out windows."

during air-raid drills. They helped pile up sandbags to protect buildings that were considered a prime target for enemy attacks.

By fall of 1941 more women were working in defense industries. In the article "Women in Democracy's Arsenal," which appeared in *The New York Times Magazine* two months before Pearl Harbor, Frank S. Adams wrote, "As American industry shifts into high gear in its drive to make this country truly the arsenal of democracy, women are beginning to play an important part in the armament plants of the nation." Adams continued to list the jobs women were already doing, including building dive bombers, making time fuses for high-explosive shells, turning out millions of rounds of machine-gun and small-arms ammunition, inspecting aircraft engines, and making rubber flotation bags for planes forced down at sea. Adams also presented Professor Johnson O'Connor's research findings of ways women surpass men, including powers of observation, number memory, accounting skills, and finger dexterity.

Despite Adams's glowing report, there were still widespread objections to hiring women. And not just from male bosses. Husbands were opposed, too. "I don't want my wife to take a man's job as long as I am still able to work for our living," one husband wrote in a letter to a newspaper. According to another husband, "I never let my wife work, and I know she is a far sweeter woman than many women who have been coarsened by having to get out in the business world. I say, let's keep the women out of industry and out of the war."

Many married women agreed. They felt that they had enough work to do as housewives. Dot remembers her mother saying that she had her "hands full taking care of a husband, a house, and two children." Women also worried that defense work was too heavy, too dirty, too dangerous, and not a place for a woman. According to a woman who finally did get a war job, "When I first started to work in the shop, I was sort of ashamed of it. My mother had always wanted me to do office work."

In January 1942, a month after Pearl Harbor, FDR called for the production of 60,000 planes, 45,000 tanks, 20,000 antiaircraft guns, and 8 million tons of merchant shipping. For 1943, FDR wanted 125,000 planes, 75,000 tanks, 35,000 antiaircraft guns, and 10 million tons of merchant shipping. And that was just part of what was needed to fight a war that spread from Asia to Europe and

Well-known singer Lena Horne "conserves gas" in an advertisement encouraging Americans to do the same for the war effort. Note the traditional feminine image portrayed in the kitchen. Many men had trouble imagining their wives working anywhere else.

North Africa. "It must be done and we have undertaken to do it," said FDR.

Industries geared up for massive wartime production. Factories were converted from making peacetime to wartime products. They changed from making sewing machines to bombs, vacuum cleaners to machine guns, shirts to mosquito netting, and kitchen sinks to cartridge cases. The Kleenex company switched to making two-gun and four-gun .50-caliber machine-gun mounts.

On February 10, 1942, the last new automobile that would be produced until the war ended in 1945 rolled off the assembly line. For the duration of the war, auto plants produced tanks, jeeps, and all kinds of weapons. At the cost of $65 million, which the U.S. government paid, the Ford Motor Company constructed a new half-mile-long building for the production of bombers. At the height of production, one bomber was produced every hour, twenty-four hours a day, seven days a week. Other new factories were built: the Pratt and Whitney Aircraft Company built a huge new plant in Longmeadow, Massachusetts, to produce crankshafts, links, propeller shafts, and master rods for aircraft engines. New shipyards were built and old ones were expanded.

Elsie Rossio remembers how her "very small, very quiet farming community" of Seneca, Illinois, was transformed: "In early 1942 we began hearing rumors that a shipyard was coming to Seneca, but many of us did not really believe it until one morning we were awakened in the wee hours by the sound of huge trucks moving down Main Street. Just a few days later, the sound of jackhammers and the rat-a-tat-tat of carpenters' hammers began echoing day and night. The site of the shipyards and dock was at the southeast corner of town on the banks of the Illinois River, but you could hear the jackhammers everywhere." The first ship was completed five months after the shipyard was built on the pastures. According to an article in the *New York Times* with the headline "Welder Launches Tank-Landing Ship," seven thousand people attended the launching, and "Mrs. Harriet Williamson, 30 years old, widowed mother of three little

With automobiles out of production until the end of the war, the Goodyear Tire and Rubber Company in Akron, Ohio, produced blimp envelopes.

girls, who learned welding and helped build the ship, smashed a bottle of champagne against the vessel. Her husband was killed in a munitions plant explosion. In recognition of her courage, the company and fellow-employees gave her and the children war bonds, a medal, and other awards, besides giving her the role of honor at today's launching."

America's industrial mobilization would require a staggering number of workers for traditionally male jobs at a time when millions of men were leaving the home front for the battlefront. So it was just a matter of time before America would be forced to deal with its entrenched attitudes about women's roles and capabilities.

FIVE

The First Six Months
"Jobs, Jobs, Jobs"

During the first six months after America's entry into the war, the Allies took a beating. The Japanese gained control of Hong Kong, Singapore, Malaya, Burma, and Thailand and were advancing toward Australia. The German army was marching toward Stalingrad and what was left of the Russian army. German general Erwin Rommel was unchecked in North Africa, and German U-boats controlled the North Atlantic.

To fight the war, huge numbers of men were drafted into or enlisted in the armed forces. "I would say within six months there were maybe twenty or thirty men left in Department 16 [Vega Aircraft Company] where maybe there had been fifteen hundred. One by one they disappeared," recalls Juanita Loveless, who had gotten a job as a riveter at Vega Aircraft in California.

As the men left, their jobs were filled by men who were exempt from the armed forces for a variety of reasons, including being too young or too old for the military. People with disabilities were also hired because employers figured they wouldn't be drafted. By 1943 almost 200,000 people with disabilities were working in war industries, up from 27,703 in 1940. Early in the war, one employer said, "In our plant we have several paralysis victims who cannot walk far or well but whose finger dexterity on assembly is excellent. We also have a blind girl who is doing a splendid job of gauging automatic screw machine parts." Supreme Engineering Corporation, a small defense plant, only hired people with disabilities and more than 95 percent of the employees were in wheelchairs. In some defense jobs, characteristics that were typically viewed as disabilities became an advantage. For example, "midgets" were hired to work inside the small spaces in airplane wings. As the war continued, employers began hiring soldiers who had been disabled and discharged. One-armed veterans were employed as welders and veterans with one leg became drill-press operators.

Prisoners also worked for the war effort after the U.S. Attorney

A blind woman worker loading primers into cartridge cases at Ogden Arsenal in Utah.

General ruled that they could produce war goods in prison factories and workshops, thus adding the labor of about 125,000 prisoners and machines worth $50 million to the work-force. At San Quentin, a maximum-security prison in California, prisoners began making submarine nets and nightsticks.

Older men were brought out of retirement to work for the war effort. In Maine, one hundred retired ship carpenters ranging from sixty to eighty years of age were hired to build wooden minesweepers. Younger workers knew about working with steel but not about working with wood or using certain tools such as the adz, a cutting tool used to shape wood.

Although at first there was a lot of discrimination against older women, they were finally hired, too. According to one older woman who wanted a full-time job, "The specter of age reared its ugly head whenever I struck out in the direction of an employment office. . . . A little later, however, it became evident that the supply of acceptable young workers would soon become exhausted. . . . Sure enough, before long . . . the age limit rose from forty to forty-five, forty-five to fifty; and then in the more congested factory districts it disappeared altogether."

Among the first women who responded to the need for war workers were those who were already working, but in low-paying jobs. Margarita Salazar quit her job in a beauty shop and got a job in an aircraft plant. "The money was in defense. You made more hours, and the more hours you made, the more money you made. And it was exciting. . . . You figured you were doing something for your country—and at the same time making money."

In 1942 so many women left low-paying jobs working in laundries that six hundred laundries were forced out of business.

An older woman worker performs the telephone "drop test." She checks for proper assembly by dropping each phone from varying heights and listening for a ring. Older women often had difficulty finding jobs before the war.

Restaurants closed, too, as waitresses left for higher-paying jobs. Schools had a hard time keeping teachers. In Vancouver, Washington, a woman teacher earned seventy-five cents an hour. As a shipyard worker, she earned one dollar and twenty-five cents an hour.

Between 1940 and 1944, more than half the women in Mobile, Alabama, who had been employed before the war changed their jobs—not surprising considering that in a week a woman shipyard worker earned $37, a salesclerk earned $21, and a waitress earned $14.

This typical wartime advertisement originally ran in the Daily Hampshire Gazette *on Tuesday, December 8, 1942.*

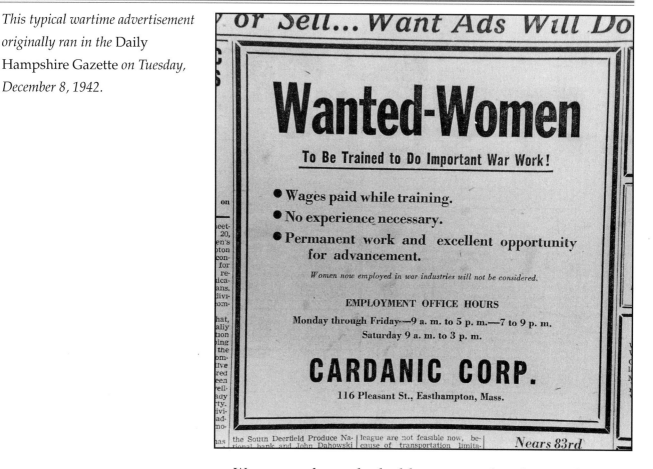

Women workers who had been unemployed since the Great Depression also jumped at the chance to get a war job. Peggy Terry later recalled, "The first work I had after the Depression was at a shell-loading plant in Viola, Kentucky. . . . They were large shells: antiaircraft, incendiaries, and tracers. We painted red on the tips of the tracers. My mother, my sister, and I worked there. Each of us worked a different shift because we had little ones at home. We made the fabulous sum of thirty-two dollars a week. To us it was just an absolute miracle. Before that, we made nothing."

But still more workers were needed as the armed forces continued to increase their demands for men. In addition, large numbers of new jobs were being created as American industry went into high gear. Factories operated round the clock seven days a week.

Newspapers printed stories with headlines such as "Millions of Women Must Be Shifted to War Work." Factories ran advertisements aimed at women. According to Juanita Loveless, "They were recruiting for any kind of work you wanted. Newspapers just splashed everywhere 'Help Wanted,' 'Help Wanted,' 'Jobs,' 'Jobs,' 'Jobs.'"

Radio stations broadcast the appeals for workers. LueRayne Culbertson later recalled hearing again and again, "If you're an American citizen, come to gate so-and-so at Lockheed or at the shipyards in San Pedro. It was just the times, when everybody went to the shipyards. It was 'We need you.' You turned the radio on: 'We need you!'"

Women responded to the appeals for a variety of reasons. Josephine von Miklos quit her job as a fashion designer to work in a munitions factory because she wanted to "pitch in and fight, too." Shirley Hackett had to "make more money because I was on my own . . . so I applied for a job at a war plant." Nell Conley got a job in a shipyard because "I had a good friend who was going to go there, and we decided, why not? We both had to work, we both had children, so we became welders, and if I may say so, damned good ones."

Adele Erenberg quit her job as a cosmetics clerk in a drugstore and got a job making hydraulic-valve systems for B-17 bombers because it seemed "asinine . . . to be selling lipstick when the country was at war. I felt that I was capable of doing something more than that toward the war effort." Terry Gianzinetti, who was a child during the war, remembers that her mother felt strongly about doing her part. "My father told her, 'No. Absolutely not.

"Shorty" Johnston, the first woman to sign up with an airline as an A&E (aircraft and engine) mechanic, checks the firewall installation of an American Airlines Flagship.

You're not going to work!' So she talked an employer into letting her bring home parts to assemble, and started her own home-based industry. My father was so angry, but in the end he turned out to be very proud of her."

In early 1942 the Bureau of Labor Statistics predicted a shortage of some six million workers by late 1943. In April, FDR created the War Manpower Commission (WMC), headed by Paul V. McNutt, "to assure the most effective mobilization and

A woman gas burner for a shipbuilding company. Note her oversized gloves, which were probably men's gloves.

maximum utilization of the nation's manpower in the prosecution of the war."

Because of several government studies, the WMC knew that manpower had to become womanpower on a massive scale to maintain full production of war matériel. As one study put it, "With the exception of the few hundred thousand boys of predraft age, this gap [of workers] will have to be plugged almost entirely by women—mostly by women who have never before

A cartoon that originally appeared in the Daily Hampshire Gazette *on Saturday, January 9, 1943. It shows the War Manpower Commission's Paul McNutt, with a woman war worker as Miss America 1943. This year he measures her strength—not her beauty.*

been gainfully employed and who are not driven to seek work by economic necessity."

In developing its "program for utilization of women workers," the WMC decided not to make "special efforts" to recruit married women with young children because the "first responsibility of women in war as in peace is to provide suitable care for their young children." But just in case it turned out that married women with young children were needed, the WMC also stated as its official policy that "Barriers against the employment of women with young children should not be set up by employers. The decision as to gainful employment should in all cases be an individual decision made by the woman herself in the light of the particular conditions prevailing in her home."

The WMC knew that it had to overcome long-standing, entrenched attitudes and practices to "sell" war jobs to women who had never worked outside the home before, and to their husbands, bosses, and coworkers. The WMC gained a powerful ally when FDR created the Office of War Information (OWI) in June. Headed by Elmer H. Davis, the OWI was set up "to coordinate the dissemination of war information by means of the press, radio, and motion pictures."

In other words, the OWI was in charge of propaganda (an effort to influence public opinion), a word that is rarely used today in a positive way. However, Elmer Davis appeared to have high hopes when he announced "This is a people's war, and to win it the people should know as much about it as they can. This office will do its best to tell the truth and nothing but the truth."

Throughout the war the OWI produced a blizzard of press releases, pamphlets, posters, and photographs. One widely published photograph showed two sturdy women in work clothes, hands in their pockets, standing beside a locomotive and talking to each other with obvious pleasure. According to the caption: "American women fight on home front in U.S. industries: two American girls, employed as war workers by a big American railroad, enjoy a moment of relaxation after cleaning and preparing the locomotive. . . . These girls, like millions of other American women, left homes, schools, and pleasanter occupations to work on U.S. railroads, in shipyards, steel plants and war industries to release more men for U.S. fighting forces."

November 1942: The Office of War Information (OWI) news bureau.

The OWI had several bureaus, including a magazine bureau, which sent a bimonthly guide, the *Magazine War Guide*, to magazine and newspaper writers and editors and radio reporters throughout the United States. The *Magazine War Guide* listed war topics that might be featured in newspapers and magazines or discussed on the radio. The guide provided details about how to discuss each topic and included such suggestions as "Fiction stories of any kind, set in these industries [steel, coal, copper, lead, zinc, lumber] help considerably in showing their importance to the war [and] the interdependence of the armed forces and the workmen and workwomen who make the weapons."

Periodically the *Magazine War Guide* would include a supplement such as the *War Guide* supplement for *Love* and

Western Love magazines. In one supplement writers and editors were encouraged to write stories that might help men accept women as coworkers: "This can be done through stories showing the advent of women in logging camps, on the railroads, riding the ranges, and showing them not as weak sisters but as coming through in manly style."

For the duration of the war the OWI worked closely with the WMC on devising ways to recruit women into war production. They also focused on convincing employers to hire women. Although an increasing number of male employers appeared willing to hire women, others still refused. In fact, in the first months after Pearl Harbor only 80,000 women were hired out of the estimated 750,000 who had applied for work at war plants.

Almost a year after Pearl Harbor, employers, such as the Todd Shipyard Corporation hired women after being told by government officials that men in semi-skilled jobs would lose their deferment from the draft within six months. In response to advertisements for women to work at the Todd Erie Basin Dry Dock in Brooklyn, New York, and the Todd Hoboken Dry Dock in Hoboken, New Jersey, 3,500 women applied by letter. Actresses, housewives, nurses, and recent college graduates applied. One actress wrote, "Perhaps you might feel that I could do a good job of entertaining the soldiers in camps. But there are others who are better entertainers than I. I gladly give way to them. But I feel that I must do something to help, and it seems to me that an opportunity to work in a shipyard is almost heaven-sent." A woman who had been a housewife for twenty-seven years wrote that her two sons were in the service. She wanted to work so that she "would not sit home feeling sorry" for herself. Another housewife wrote about her son in the navy, "My Bill will be in the

A recruitment poster from 1942 shows a woman war worker saluting American soldiers. Note the "V for Victory" emblem on her cap.

fighting; and the time I spend helping him will never tire me." Elinore M. Herrick, who had recently been hired as the shipyard's personnel director, said that an "astonishing" number of older women applied. Of the 3,500 women who had applied, seventy were selected to be interviewed, and twenty-six were hired and were soon known as "shipyardettes."

The OWI and WMC were assisted by the War Advertising Council (WAC), a voluntary group of advertising executives. The WAC had been created in 1941 by people in the advertising industry who were worried that advertising might not be considered useful during wartime. The WAC stressed its value to the war effort by asserting that "We have within our hands the greatest aggregate means of mass education and persuasion the world has ever seen."

Like the advertisers, a group of leading writers also formed an organization, the Writers' War Board. Organized by Rex Stout, a popular mystery writer, the Writers' War Board stated that the writers were "united in the belief that the board should furnish wholehearted support of any measures which the government considers necessary to a speedy and complete victory over the Axis." In particular, the Writers' War Board worked closely with the OWI to develop and write stories designed to recruit women.

In June 1942 the OWI finally released some good war news. "A stupendous naval victory is in the making," read the message from Admiral Chester W. Nimitz that was distributed to the press and radio. On June 7, exactly six months after Pearl Harbor, Americans learned that the U.S. Navy had won the Battle of Midway and ended the Japanese threat to Hawaii and to the U.S. mainland. Although Americans were heartened, they knew that the end of the war was a long way off. Axis troops were

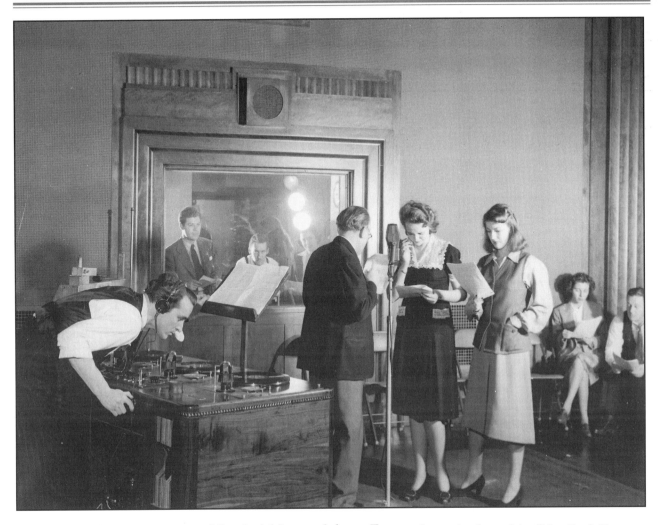

entrenched from Norway to North Africa and from France to western Russia. In the Pacific, Japanese control stretched from the Netherlands East Indies to parts of the Aleutian Islands. To keep their spirits up, Dot Chastney and her friends kept reassuring each other. "We repeated all the things we heard the adults say. 'Our country is bigger. . . . We're stronger. . . . We've never lost a war. . . . God is on our side.'" Helping the war effort made Dot and her friends feel better.

In the spring of 1942, Dot and her classmates knit squares to make afghans for the Red Cross to distribute. "Our teacher set

A rehearsal for "You Can't Do Business with Hitler," a radio show written and produced by the OWI radio section.

aside a time in the school week—knitting time—and the girls taught the boys to knit. It was really fun because some of the boys couldn't get the hang of knitting. It gave us a little power over the boys. We could say to them, 'But your square is so uneven.' They were good sports about it because everyone felt that we were doing this for the war effort," says Dot.

That theme—doing this for the war effort—was what the WMC and OWI used again and again to recruit women war workers. The question was: Could they recruit enough women to do traditionally male jobs?

SIX

The War Wears On
"I'll do anything for my country."

By the summer of 1942 there was some talk about drafting women into the labor force. Britain required its women to register to work. So did Russia. Several bills to establish a draft for women were introduced in the U.S. Congress. The American public seemed to support the idea. According to a Gallup poll, 68 percent of people surveyed answered yes to the question "Would you be in favor of starting now to draft single women between the ages of 21 and 35 to train them for wartime jobs?"

One of the arguments against a nationwide draft for women was the fear of intensifying the problems that were arising from the major migration of people that was under way. During the war, perhaps as many as twenty million people left their homes for one reason or another. Throughout America people were on the move, going to military camps or looking for work. Half the black agricultural workers in the rural South moved to urban areas in search of high-paying jobs. Within three and a half years more than seven million women changed their address to a different county.

"For my husband and I to both have jobs, we had to go to an industrial section of the nation, so we moved to East St. Louis, Missouri," explains Frankie Cooper, who got a job as a molder's helper, "the dirtiest job anyone can imagine."

People traveled any way they could—by train, bus, car, or

Defense housing in Erie, Pennsylvania. Each trailer housed up to four people and sat on a plot of ground measuring 25 feet by 50 feet. Each was equipped with a gas stove, an icebox, and davenport beds, while toilets, showers, and laundry facilities were located in the central utility building shown at the right of the trailers.

hitching a ride. "In those days they had drivers' cars who came back and forth. You'd pay something like ten dollars or fifteen dollars. There were six or seven passengers, and we were stacked on top of each other," recalls Juanita Loveless.

As the migration continued, areas of the country with war plants were swamped with newcomers. The population soared in such boom cities as Seattle, Washington; Detroit, Michigan; Mobile, Alabama; and Buffalo, New York. In the first two years of the war, Burbank, California, grew from 12,000 to 60,000 people.

In Mobile, Alabama, more than 80,000 workers arrived in 1942. Six communities were built in eighteen months to house shipyard workers in the Vancouver, Washington, area. They were called Ogden Meadows, Burton Homes, Fruit Valley, McLaughlin Heights, Bagley Downs, and Harney Hills.

After the shipyard was built in Seneca, Illinois, the population went from 1,235 to 6,500 within a few months, and eventually grew to 27,000. The shipyards and aircraft plants in California attracted as many as 1.4 million people.

The huge influx of people to places such as these created enormous problems—housing shortages, overburdened schools, inefficient public transportation systems, and inadequate sanitation facilities. Under these circumstances, policymakers

A "Westcraft home" built by Western Trailer Company. Prefabricated houses, such as the one pictured above, were used as temporary housing for war workers in overpopulated areas.

decided not to draft women but to recruit the ones who already lived in areas with labor shortages.

According to an August 15, 1942, report in *Business Week*, "Between 44,000 and 60,000 additional workers will be needed in war industries in Seattle by the end of 1942. And the city wants to find as many as possible right at home, because its population has increased by more than 110,000 during the last two years, and the housing situation is acute."

In August 1942, the United States Employment Service (USES), which was supervised by the WMC, conducted voluntary registration drives as a strategy to get women war workers. The drives included carefully planned newspaper and radio publicity filled with patriotic messages. In Detroit, which needed 80,000 new women workers before November, the USES distributed 600,000 registration cards to households in the Detroit area. Women were asked to fill out the cards with information about their education, work experience, children, and job preference. The USES analyzed the information and assigned willing women to jobs or training programs. Other drives were held: in Seattle, Washington, 6,000 women signed up with the USES; in Oregon, 90,000 women registered to work, although they indicated that they would rather help harvest crops than work in a factory; and in Northampton, Massachusetts, a small town surrounded by defense plants, 4,215 women registered to do war work. While filling out their cards, some women wrote comments in the margins, including: "My husband is in Australia and I want to help make weapons for him and his buddies." "I regard it as a duty to my country to do whatever will be helpful." "I'll do anything my country wants to help lick the Japs and Nazis."

While registration drives for women workers were being held

on the home front, soldiers were taking the offensive on the battlefront. On August 7, 1942, U.S. Marines landed on Guadalcanal in the Solomon Islands in the Pacific Ocean and began the first offensive action in the war against Japan. On November 8, Allied forces invaded North Africa. On November 19, Russian troops launched a counterattack against German troops occupying Stalingrad. After months of fierce fighting, the Marines gained control of Guadalcanal and the German soldiers in Russia surrendered, as did the German army in Africa. By late 1942, Americans were beginning to feel that the Allies would win the war.

But a lot of fighting lay ahead: Japanese troops controlled a significant portion of Southeast Asia. German troops still controlled most of Europe and parts of Russia, and German U-boat activity had taken a heavy toll on merchant ships carrying foodstuffs, men, and war matériel that were headed for British and Russian ports.

Dot Chastney remembers going to the New Jersey seashore and seeing "the oil from a torpedoed oil tanker washing in on the sand." Jackie Brock, who was a child during the war, remembers being at a picnic on a beach in Florida. "My father was looking through his binoculars and saw a German submarine. He told me and my mother to act normal because if he could see the submarine, the men on the submarine could see us." After acting "normal" and eating their food, Jackie and her parents left. Her father reported the submarine to military authorities. Jackie later recalled, "I don't know if it was the same sub, but the next day there was a report in the newspaper about a German sub being sunk off the Florida shore."

Huge amounts of war matériel would be needed to continue

Women "groom" the transparent noses of A-20 attack bombers. The patterns seen on the noses are reflections of the ceiling lights.

the offensive and win the war. However, as 1943 approached, the labor shortage was beginning to slow down production. Drafting women workers was not an option, and registration drives had not recruited enough women. In addition, there were still employers who refused to hire women.

Faced with this labor emergency, the WMC and the OWI decided to increase the propaganda campaign. Posters were produced with slogans such as: "Women in the war: We can't win without them." The OWI joined in and sent photographs of women war workers to magazines and newspapers. There were

The following OWI caption appeared with this photo in 1943: "Kathryn M. Miller, first woman to be employed as a laborer at the Reading Company general stores. . . . She is a former hosiery mill employee and says she doesn't mind the cold at all."

photographs of women riveting, working on airplane motors, and installing fixtures and assemblies to a tail fuselage section of a B-17 bomber.

Writers who worked for the OWI wrote captions for the photographs that conveyed a variety of messages. Some captions simply described the photograph: "Boeing aircraft plant, Seattle, Wash. Dec. 1942. Production of B-17 F [Flying fortress] bombing planes. Two women working on a machine." Or, "Nashville,

Tenn. Aug. 1942. Girl riveter in the bomber fuselage at the Vultee aircraft corporation plant." Other captions provided some information about the job the women were doing: "De Soto bomber plant, Detroit, Mich. Oct. 1942. Girls dipping magnesium tubing in hot clean bath to get rid of grease and acid." Another group of captions contained sales pitches such as: "Paterson, N.J. 1942. Emily Rabbat making parts for airplane engines on a horizontal milling machine at a Wright Aeronautical corporation plant. She formerly worked in a silk mill. With modern machine tools, the work is clean, safe, and requires little physical effort." Or, "Lititz, Penna. Nov. 1942. Emma Dougherty, who does a man's work for a man's pay, cleaning out her end grinding machine."

Magazine articles were published to entice women to take war jobs. In November 1942 the very popular magazine *Reader's Digest* reprinted an upbeat article, "Ma's Making Bombers!" The author of the article, Elisabeth Meyer, wrote about single women, married women, mothers, and grandmothers doing everything from installing exhaust pipes in planes to riveting and finishing bomb doors. Meyer visited working women throughout America: "In low, vast airplane plants squatting in the wheat fields of Kansas or melting into the orange groves of California; in three-story factories in the East and the Middle West and battered machine shops in New England; in the open-air clangor of the giant Pacific Coast shipyards, I saw the women working." Also in 1942, a nationwide contest was held to select "Miss Victory, the Typical American War Worker." Ann Vickery was one of the twelve sectional winners. "I've never been tardy or absent from work," she declared during an interview.

For Christmas of 1942, Dot's teachers decided that it would be nice to send Christmas cards to all the former students of their school who were in the armed forces. "So they had a little contest to select the design and verse for the card. My drawing won and my very best girlfriend, Eileen Ellinger's, verse won," remembers Dot, who still has several of the Christmas cards fifty years later. More than eighty men and a few women in the armed forces received the cards. "I was so proud," says Dot.

SEVEN

The Final War Years
"It's a man's and woman's world."

By the end of 1942 the situation had improved for the American military. However, American industry continued to be desperately short of workers. Four million new workers would be needed in 1943 to maintain full production. Child labor laws had been suspended for the duration of the war, and millions of children between the ages of twelve and seventeen were employed. All the available men were either in the military or already employed. So were all of the women who had worked before the war and the single women who had been recently recruited to join the workforce. Some housewives were taking war jobs, but most housewives had not yet responded to the appeals for war workers. And they were the largest potential source of workers left in the United States. WMC head Paul V. McNutt stated, "Getting these women to go into industry is a tremendous sales proposition."

During 1943 and 1944, the WMC and OWI launched two massive campaigns to sell war jobs to housewives. And they decided to appeal to patriotism. Posters appeared everywhere, each with a different slogan in large letters: "We soldiers of supply pledge that our fighting men will not want!" "Do the job he left behind: Apply U.S. Employment Service." "On the job we must all do our best, can't you see; for our boys' very lives rest with you and me. . . ."

One poster featured a picture of a woman holding a wrench

A recruitment poster from 1944.

and working on machinery at a table with the slogan "You bet I'm fighting too! What kind of Americans would we be if we let anyone rob us of our Liberty?"

Short advertisement films aimed at potential women workers were made by the government and industry. The films were widely shown at movie theaters throughout the United States. They were also shown at churches, civic organizations, schools, and colleges.

Curtiss Wright Aeronautical, manufacturer of the Wright Cyclone engine that was used in military planes, hired the world-famous broadcaster Lowell Thomas to narrate a series of advertisement films. The films' titles included: *Back Sons in Service; Team Up to Beat Axis;* and *Wife Makes Minutes Count.* Each film begins with Thomas seated behind an official-looking desk. In his deep, distinctive voice, Thomas informs viewers that "Wright is in the fight until the last shot is fired . . . and so should you."

The patriotism, however, was presented in ways that reinforced women's traditional images and roles. A Seattle newspaper article warned women not to "go berserk over the new opportunities for masculine clothing and mannish actions." Women workers at the navy yard were told to be "feminine and ladylike, even though you are filling a man's shoes." At Boeing Aircraft, the Women's Recreational Activity Council offered courses in proper dress, makeup, poise, and personality to help women workers maintain their "FQ" (Femininity Quotient). In an

A photograph showing newly developed attire for women workers at Allis-Chalmers Manufacturing Company in Milwaukee, Wisconsin. The following caption accompanied the photo: "Denim overalls, cotton knit shirt (cooler & easier to launder). Cap to cover all of the hair. Closed toe oxfords, firm support (re-enforced toe where danger of dropping objects on foot). Safety goggles with metal side shields (goggles required on all machine work)."

This postcard of Wendy the Welder presented a less glamorized image of women war workers. In real life, Wendy the Welder was Janet Doyle, a worker at the Kaiser Richmond Liberty Shipyards in California.

WENDY THE WELDER

advertisement for electric companies, the description of a woman worker was, "She's 5 feet 1 from her 4A slippers to her spun-gold hair. She loves flower hats, veils, smooth orchestras—and being kissed by a boy who's now in North Africa. But man oh man, how she can handle her huge and heavy press!"

When Edna Slocum was named the "Welding Queen" in California, news reports included information about how she managed to be a welder and a housewife who still had "time for a [hair] wave."

In an article in the widely read *Life* magazine, the writer described Marguerite Kershner, who worked at Boeing Aircraft: "Now, at day's end, her hands may be bruised, there's grease under her nails, her makeup is smudged, and her curls out of place. When she checks in the next morning at 6:30 A.M., her hands will be smooth, her nails polished, her makeup and curls in order, for Marguerite is neither drudge nor slave but the heroine of a new order."

In 1943, a graphic artist, J. Howard Miller, produced a poster for the Westinghouse Corporation that showed a woman worker wearing a bandana and work shirt with her employee identification button pinned on the collar. Her right arm is bent and her hand is in a fist. Above her head are the words "We Can Do It!" She is portrayed with fingernail polish, lipstick, rouge, plucked eyebrows, and mascara. Since the 1970s, this poster has been mistakenly labeled Rosie the Riveter and has been

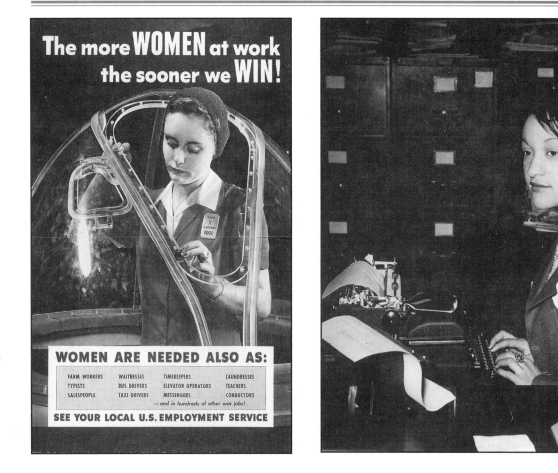

A recruitment poster (above) *showing a woman at work on an airplane. Several "essential civilian war jobs" are also posted.*
A clerical worker in Washington, D.C. (above right). *A bank teller in Worcester, Massachusetts* (opposite left). *Police officers at Hunters Point* (opposite right).

reprinted on posters, magazine covers, and many other items.

Propaganda aimed at women workers presented war jobs as similar to housework. In *Glamour Girl '43*, a short film showing women doing war jobs, a male narrator smoothly reassures viewers that "instead of cutting the lines of a dress, this woman cuts the pattern of aircraft parts. Instead of baking cake, this woman is cooking gears to reduce the tension in the gears after use . . . a lathe holds no more terror than a sewing machine. . . . After a short apprenticeship, this woman can operate a drill press just as easily as a juice extractor in her own kitchen." In one scene the hands of a woman filing her nails are shown alongside a picture of an industrial file.

Large numbers of women entered the workforce—almost three million—in 1943. But still more women were needed. And not just in defense plants. Women were also needed in "essential civilian" jobs—jobs that kept the home front running smoothly: teachers, telephone operators, taxi and bus drivers, child-care workers, restaurant workers, bank tellers, clerical workers, grocery store clerks, police officers, and hospital workers.

In September 1943 the WMC launched its biggest recruitment effort to date, the "Women in Necessary Services" campaign, which was aimed at recruiting women for "essential civilian" jobs. Prior to the war, some of the "essential civilian" jobs like bank tellers and grocery store clerks had been traditionally filled by men.

Restaurant and hospital work had been traditionally done by women, but the women workers had left them for higher-paying factory jobs. Other jobs such as child care and clerical jobs had multiplied because of the war. A poster was produced that showed four smiling women in front of an American flag. The caption simply read: "Secretaries of War." Another poster had the slogan "Soldiers Without Guns" and showed a woman seated at a typewriter in front of a woman welder and a woman factory worker.

These "essential civilian" jobs were harder to sell because they had lower pay and status. So the WMC and OWI intensified their efforts and ran a special campaign. As the OWI's magazine bureau explained the problem to editors and writers: "By and large, women do not view work of this kind as war work . . . The time has come for them to realize how urgently they are needed—to keep the wheels of our civilian economy turning during the war period." To sell this type of work to women, editors and writers were told that "these jobs will have to be glorified as patriotic war service if American women are to be persuaded to take them and stick to them." A very popular writer, Dorothy Parker, did just that in a widely read article that she wrote, "Are We Women or Are We Mice?" According to Parker, "Somewhere, right near you, there is an empty job that must be filled; a job a man has left to go where he was told to go. He may have driven a bus, a taxi, or a trolley; he may have been a conductor or have stood behind a ticket window; he may have worked in a bank, a drugstore, or a telegraph office. If he can do what he is doing now, certainly you can do what he used to do. For God's sake—are we women or are we mice? . . . There won't be any chic uniforms. . . . There won't be farewell parties when you set forth to war. . . . [But] you will be doing great work in the greatest of works . . . the saving of the future."

In addition to recruiting women to take defense and "essential civilian" jobs, the WMC and OWI still had to persuade some male employers to hire women workers. Some employers preferred to produce less or even turn down a contract for war goods if it meant hiring women workers.

In 1943 the War Department joined in the campaign to persuade male employers. They distributed a booklet, "You're Going to Employ Women." The booklet advised employers about hiring, training, and supervising women. According to the booklet, "In some respects women workers are superior to men. *Properly hired, properly trained, properly handled,* new women employees are splendidly efficient workers. The desire of a new woman worker to help win the war—to shorten it even by a minute—gives her an enthusiasm that more than offsets industrial inexperience."

Women on line enter work at Boeing. Note the sign that says WOMEN ONLY. Women and men were separated at Boeing because women's purses were opened and checked, and it was considered unacceptable for the men to see the women's personal belongings.

To help employers, the WMC ran programs to train women to do war work and programs to train foremen and male supervisors to work with women. Employers were also told how to adapt machines to make them easier for women workers to operate. Extension levers were added so that machines could be operated with finger strength. Conveyor belts were installed to eliminate the need to carry heavy items. Safety devices were installed. Several experts agreed with the comment in *Fortune* magazine: "Many such aids should have been developed for men long ago anyway, and plants are going to operate faster and more efficiently with them after the war is over."

The propaganda paid attention to husbands, too. One WMC booklet, "Answers to Questions Women Ask About War Work," included a picture of a seated woman, her teenage daughter standing behind her, talking with her pipe-smoking husband. The booklet tells women: "If your husband understands clearly how urgently you are needed and how much you can contribute toward saving the lives of loved ones now in the armed forces, he will help you work out your home problems." A poster produced by the WMC shows a woman wearing overalls and a scarf with a man beside her. They are standing in front of an American flag and his hands are on her shoulders. The slogan reads: "I'm proud . . . my husband wants me to do my part: See your U.S. Employment Service."

Throughout 1943 and 1944, an incredible range of job opportunities for women continued to open up everywhere. One male bastion after another opened its door. And women streamed through.

Prior to the war, conductors of symphony orchestras, all of whom were men, had refused to hire women musicians. The

I'm Proud... my husband *wants* me to do my part

SEE YOUR U. S. EMPLOYMENT SERVICE
WAR MANPOWER COMMISSION

conductors said that women did not have the stamina or the temperament to play in an orchestra. However, they changed their tune when large numbers of male musicians left for the military or took much higher paying defense jobs. By 1944, only three of the top orchestras in the country were male-only: the New York Philharmonic and the symphonies in Minneapolis and Boston. The symphony in Houston held the record with twenty-six women players, including a woman concertmaster. The St. Louis symphony had five women, including an oboist and a

Two wartime women's ball teams line up in the "V for Victory" formation during "The Star-Spangled Banner."

woman "bull fiddle player." Sixteen women were hired for the Kansas City orchestra, including a tympanist whom the conductor recruited from a band where she had been playing the snare drums. The Seattle symphony had twenty-one women; there were eighteen in Pittsburgh, seventeen in New Orleans, and twelve in Los Angeles.

And there were other opportunities for women. The U.S. Department of Agriculture hired women to work in a sawmill at Turkey Pond, near Concord, New Hampshire. Florence Drouin and Elizabeth Esty were "pond women." Their job was to stand on a log raft floating in the pond. Using their logging pikes, Drouin and Esty steered other logs into place on the slip in the sawmill. From there Dorothy De Greenia, a "slip woman," would roll the logs to the rack that held them until the logs headed toward the main saw.

Opportunities also opened up for professional women. In August 1943 *Newsweek* reported that "Uppity though they had once been about accepting women doctors in the armed services, the War and Navy Department last week about-faced with a vengeance. The Army launched a drive for 10,000 additional physicians . . . and frankly included in that number all the women they could get. The Navy welcomed the ladies even more." On the home front, Harvard Medical School finally admitted women. Hospitals throughout the country opened their doors to women doctors.

While women doctors were making employment gains, so were women lawyers, astronomers, architects, geologists, engineers, journalists, and meteorologists. Women chemists were in demand, too. Between 1941 and 1944, the staff of women chemists jumped 500 percent at the Mellon Institute of Industrial

Research in Pittsburgh. At Westinghouse Research Laboratories in Pittsburgh, Elisabeth M. Ackermann, a twenty-one-year-old chemist, helped develop a new plastic glue strong enough to support the weight of a two-hundred-ton locomotive. In a press release announcing Ackermann's achievement, she was described as being "as much at home at her laboratory as a housewife in the kitchen . . . [who] prepares her favorite 'recipe.'"

In August 1944 the article "Women at Work" appeared in *National Geographic* magazine. According to the article, "The balance of power rests in women's hands. Literally. Behind the whine of sawmills and roar of blast furnaces, the hammer of arsenals and thunder of machine shops—in shipyards, factories,

Florence Drouin and Elizabeth Esty were pond women employed by the U.S. Department of Agriculture at Turkey Pond near Concord, New Hampshire.

Chemist Elisabeth Ackermann measures water condensation as her plastic glue mixture is being heated to her right.

foundries, slaughterhouses, and laboratories—women are manipulating the machinery of war." The article described the extraordinary variety of work women were doing and ended with these words: "And as the war goes on, the great feel of it and the great interdependence of it gather strength. It's a man's *and* woman's world."

However, by the end of 1944 it was clear that the war was not going to go on much longer. On June 6, known as D-Day, allied troops had invaded France and were pushing the German troops back to Germany. Just before Christmas, German and Allied troops fought a fierce battle that became known as the Battle of the Bulge. Allied troops finally triumphed, but 77,000

Allied soldiers were killed, including three young men from Dot Chastney's hometown.

Dot remembers that "they weren't the first to be killed, but three at once was too much. Everybody knew them and knew their families. They were no older than eighteen years old. It was really bad. It cast a terrible pall over the town."

In the war against Japan, U.S. troops had captured island after island in 1943 and 1944: Bougainville, Tarawa, and Guam. "I

Operating a bolt-cutting machine at Todd Erie Basin.

Boeing Aircraft plant.

knew the names and locations of all the islands," Dot remembers.

As 1945 began, the peak of industrial mobilization in America was over. Slowly the number of jobs in defense industries declined. Although more bloody fighting lay ahead, Japan and Germany were just months away from surrendering. Before 1945 ended, millions of men would return from the battlefront to the home front. And soon there would be enough male workers again. The propaganda would now be aimed at telling women war workers to return to their homes. But what about the women war workers? What had they experienced? What had they endured? And what had they felt about doing war jobs?

Welders on their way to work at Todd Erie Basin.

EIGHT

Pioneers in the American Workplace
"I had the chance to prove that I could do something."

Throughout the war years most women who took war jobs entered an alien world, a world that had always been male-only. Josephine von Miklos was the first woman to set foot in the tool-grinding room of a company that had been in business for 140 years. Shortly after she arrived, von Miklos had the following encounter with a male coworker:

> This man was standing next to me, watching me set up a somewhat intricate tool on the magnetic chuck of my grinding machine.
>
> "You're a pretty good mechanic," he said finally, and added, "for a woman."
>
> "Why for a woman?" I asked, and wished I hadn't. I knew what was coming. I had heard it a dozen times before.
>
> "Well," he said, and spat a hunk of chewing tobacco on the floor, "it ain't women's work."

But for the duration of World War II it *was* women's work, and women of all ages, races, shapes and sizes, educational achievement, and backgrounds became pioneers in the American workplace. "Physically, mentally, everything—that was tough for complete greenhorns to go out on large construction and not know what on earth you're getting into," LueRayne Culbertson later said about her experience working in a shipyard.

Inez Sauer later recalled how foreign the industrial scene was to her when she began her job handing out tools to workers in the tool room at an airplane plant: "Some man came in and asked for a bastard file. I said to him, 'If you don't control your language, you won't get any service here.' I went to my supervisor and said, 'You'll have to correct this man. I won't tolerate that kind of language.' He laughed and laughed and said, 'Don't you know what a bastard file is? It's the name of a very coarse file.' He went over and took one out and showed me."

Women learned how to do their jobs in a variety of ways. Sauer educated herself. She insisted that the company let her study

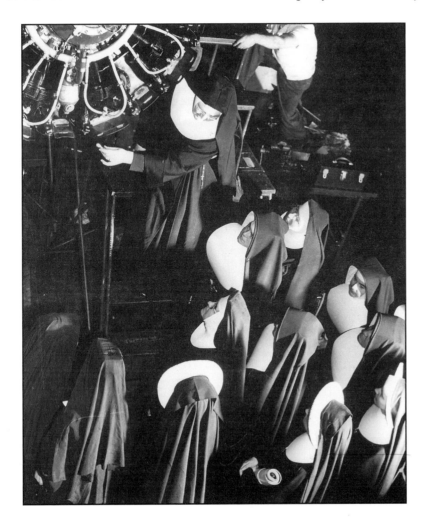

A wide variety of women received vocational training. The following caption appeared on this official OWI photo:
"Field trips for Sister Aquinas' preflight class include inspection tours of hangars at the Washington National Airport. Here, Sister Aquinas explains engine structure to her students."

Aircraft riveters at Brill Company in Philadelphia (opposite page) *celebrate the completion of their training. Janice Grant* (see arrow) *worked on the center wing section of the PBY Flying Boat (a Navy reconnaissance plane). She worked a 52-hour week and was a member of the sheet metal workers' union. Janice would later marry Stan Berenstain, then a medical artist in the army, and become Jan Berenstain. Together they would write and illustrate the well-known Berenstain Bears book series for children.*

secret material that showed all the tools and machines that were used in her plant. In addition, she also would "roam around the machine area and become acquainted with what they were doing." Rachel Wray went to school at night to learn how to read blueprints and do riveting. During the day she worked as a pastry cook. She graduated from night school in three months and was one of the first women hired at Consolidated Aircraft (Convair). "I loved working at Convair. I loved the challenge of getting dirty and getting into the work. I did one special riveting job, hand riveting that could not be done by machine. I worked on that job for three months, ten hours a day, six days a week, and slapped three-eighth- or three-quarter-inch rivets by hand that no one else would do."

Some women started working without the benefit of formal training programs. Many of the women in Wray's department got on-the-job training from her. "Our department had a majority of women. Many of them had no training at all, particularly the older women. We had women in our department who were ex-schoolteachers, artists, housewives. I'd sit them down and show them how to use the drill press, the size drill to use, the size of screw, the kind of rivets. . . . Then I would go back and check to see if the riveting was okay, and if there were any bad rivets, they had to take them out."

Training programs for women sprang up everywhere. Colleges offered courses. So did the WMC. Industries set up special training programs.

Regardless of how well trained they were, women war workers had to overcome many obstacles. Working conditions were difficult. Shirley Hackett worked in a factory that made ball bearings. She later recalled, "It was extremely dirty. There was oil

on the floor, and the area where we worked was very crowded; every inch of the plant was covered with machinery for vital work. The noise was so bad that you could not hear each other without yelling."

Factory work was also frequently dangerous. Some rivets got red-hot. In addition, women riveters often had to climb high up onto scaffolding to work on the side of a ship. The first time Virginia Wilkinson had to make a climb she asked the supervisor whether people fell off onto the concrete below. "Not often," he replied. "Just once."

Women workers were injured, disabled, and even killed in

Searching for defective bullet jackets at the Stanley plant in New Britain, Connecticut. War work was often repetitive and monotonous.

industrial accidents. On January 21, 1944, an article appeared in the *New York Times* with the following information: "Industrial casualties (women and men) between Pearl Harbor and January 1st of this year aggregated 37,500 killed, or 7,500 more than the military dead, 210,000 permanently disabled, and 4,500,000 temporarily disabled, or sixty times the number of military wounded and missing."

Josephine von Miklos described a woman who was scalped when her hair got caught in a machine that did not have a safety guard. Shirley Hackett handled steel ball bearings before they had been smoothed. Before long, the rough steel edges would tear into the heavy gloves that she wore. According to Hackett, "By the time your foreman would bring over new gloves, your hands would be bleeding all over the place. That was one thing you had to watch constantly—that you didn't cut your hands so badly you couldn't work."

Workers were also exposed to all kinds of chemicals. Peggy Terry helped fill artillery shells with a powder. "I pulled a lot of gadgets on a machine. The shell slid under and powder went into it. Another lever you pulled tamped it down. . . . You did this over and over." According to Terry, "It [the powder] turned us orange. Just as orange as orange. Our hair was streaked orange. Our hands, our face, our neck just turned orange, even our eyeballs. We never questioned. None of us ever asked, 'What is this? Is it harmful?' We simply didn't think about it. That was just one of the conditions of the job."

Women war workers also had to deal with sexual harassment. According to Shirley Hackett, some male workers would "rub against you in any way they could, try to feel or touch you." When another woman, a welder in a shipyard, refused her male boss's sexual advances, he put her out in the rain to work. She later recalled, "You were hooked up to electricity when you were welding, and because your stuff would get wet, it would shock you. And I finally got so tired of it that I finally told the foreman, and he just acted like it was all my fault."

While some women were being sexually harassed, many women were being paid less than men despite the WMC's policy

A track gang at work on the Baltimore & Ohio Railroad in New Castle, Pennsylvania. Despite newly gained independence for women, men often remained in higher positions.

of equal pay for equal work. In 1942 the Women's Bureau of the U.S. Department of Labor surveyed eighteen ammunition plants and found that only three paid women and men workers equally. In August 1942 the daily wages for "learners" for a 48-hour week at the U.S. Armory in Springfield, Massachusetts, was published in a local newspaper: "$5.28 for men, $3.36 for boys, and $3.12 for women."

According to Edna "Shorty" Hopkins, "We were doing the same kind of welding that the men were. But they didn't call ours certified. We only got $1.20. I asked, 'Am I doing certified

welding?' 'No, Shorty, you're not.' But I was, and I knew it, but there was nothing I could do."

In an effort to improve their working situation, many women joined labor unions. Some unions, such as the United Electrical Workers, helped women members by urging store owners to stay open later to meet their needs. They also backed women in their effort to get equal pay and campaigned for federal funds for child care. However, in general, unions focused on protecting male workers. In fact, some unions protested against women being hired. In Seattle an official of the Taxicab Drivers'

Taxi drivers in San Francisco. Some members of the Taxicab Drivers' Union protested the hiring of women.

Union declared that driving was "not a woman's job."

Off the job, many women war workers did double duty as housewives and mothers. And it was not easy. Women war workers generally worked six days a week and long hours each day. Getting to work was usually time-consuming because public transportation was always crowded and gas was rationed. "I don't get so tired on the job, but this bus riding wears me out," said a woman who worked at an aircraft factory. Shopping was a chore because of rationing. And if a woman war worker had young children, finding child care was not easy.

Some employers built child-care centers. Kaiser Industries built the Child Service Center for workers at its huge shipyards in Oregon. The center was open twenty-four hours a day, provided medical care, and offered many programs for children eighteen months to six years old. They also had a food service that prepared meals for workers to take home with their children.

The federal government also built child-care centers, but not enough. And some of the centers that were built were too expensive for workers and were located in places that were hard for many working mothers to reach. In addition, some women were reluctant to trust their children to child-care centers. Most working mothers relied on relatives to take care of their children. In some families, older children took care of younger children.

Regardless of what they had to deal with, most women were determined to succeed. Edna Hopkins later recalled, "One day my instructor, he comes along and he took my stinger out of my hand and raised up my hood, and the tears were just rolling down, you know, and he says, 'Edna, what in the world are you crying for?' I said, 'Just look at all these burns.' And he says, 'Well, why don't you quit if it bothers you that much?' I

Army photographer David Conover took this photograph in 1945 at Radioplane Corporation for an army magazine called Yank. *The magazine wanted to show the American soldiers "morale boosting shots of pretty girls doing their bit to help the war effort." In this photograph, nineteen-year-old Norma Jeane Baker Dougherty attaches a propeller to a drone aircraft. Note the identification badge at her waist. These photographs and others taken by Conover led Norma Jeane to a modeling and film career for which she later changed her name to Marilyn Monroe.*

said, 'No, I'm bound and determined that I'm going to do this.'"

Adele Erenberg later recalled her determination to make it in the machine shop. "It was a big room with a high ceiling and fluorescent lights, and it was very noisy. I walked in there in my overalls, and suddenly all the machines stopped and every guy in the shop just turned around and looked at me. It took, I think, two weeks before anyone even talked to me. The discrimination was indescribable. They wanted to kill me. My attitude was . . . I'm going to prove to you I can do anything you can do, and maybe

Operating a giant crane sixty feet above the floor.

better than some of you. And that's exactly the way it turned out." Before long, Erenberg was assigned to do nothing but "rework," which meant that she fixed pieces that the other workers "screwed up."

Frankie Cooper, who operated a fifty-ton crane high above the factory floor, was "almost scared to death" when she learned that she had to sand the overhead rails it ran on. Cooper had been promoted to the job in an emergency after a man operator had accidentally spilled a load of hot steel and "put a lot of lives in danger." In a previous job, Cooper had been operating a small ten-ton crane that moved gun mounts and gun barrels around. In that job, she later explained, "I had learned the language of the foundry—the sign language with which you communicate to your rigger or chainman. So they offered the job to me and I took it. Pouring steel was the hardest job in the mill, and the men said, 'It's too big a responsibility for a woman. She'll never last.' But I did. The hardest part for me was sanding the rails. The rails are what the wheels of the crane run on. They're way up in the air over the concrete floor, and they have to be sanded every eight-hour shift because if your rails get too slick, your hook will slide. . . . I thought, I can't do that. I can't look down at that concrete and maneuver this little bucket of sand. I just can't do it. And one of the men said, 'Well, that'll get her. She'll never sand them tracks.' That's what made me sand them. After that, I had to. I had to show them I could do it."

Women expressed a wide range of feelings about doing war work. Although some women planned to work only for the duration of the war, the majority of women hoped to keep their jobs. According to Margie Lacoff, a war widow and electrical helper at the Navy Yard, "I like my work so much that they'll have to fire me before I leave."

Many women were enormously proud of what they accomplished. "Some of us had our doubts at first, but now after we've gotten into it, we found it's fascinating, probably because there is so much to learn. Then, too, there's a thrill in turning out a good piece of welding," a welder in a shipyard explained. Anna Nelson, a core maker in a foundry, said, "You're proud of your work when it's done—like an artist with a picture."

Women workers also expressed newfound self-confidence. "Never thought I could do such exacting work—and I'm real proud," said an older woman who did assembly work at Benedix Friez Company in Baltimore. Rachel Wray later talked about the confidence she gained working as a riveter at Convair Aircraft: "I didn't have that kind of confidence as a kid growing up, because I didn't have that opportunity. Convair was the first time in my life that I had the chance to prove that I could do something, and I did."

Lunch break at Boeing.

NINE

Peace
*"The men had been promised their jobs
when they came back."*

Dot Chastney graduated from eighth grade in June 1945. The Germans had surrendered on May 7. "It was a school day. The principal announced the news at an assembly and dismissed school. We went home, had lunch, and went to a movie in Hackensack." Dot knew that it was just a matter of time before Japan surrendered, because the United States was "throwing all of its resources against the Japanese." She and most Americans had no inkling that the United States' resources included an atomic bomb that had been created during the war.

On August 6, the United States dropped an atomic bomb on Hiroshima. Three days later the United States dropped another atomic bomb on Nagasaki. "I just couldn't begin to comprehend it. Such a huge number of people were killed. Although we had gotten used to hearing about huge numbers of dead people, this one was different. The newspapers had pictures of the mushroom cloud and everyone talked about *the* atomic bomb," says Dot. FDR had died in April, and the new president, Harry Truman, announced that the atomic bomb was "a harnessing of the basic power of the universe."

Dot was hoping that the Japanese would surrender on her fourteenth birthday, August 19. However, it happened a few days earlier, on August 14. Within three weeks, on September 2, 1945, the Allies and Japanese signed the formal surrender agreement. World War II had officially ended.

August 14, 1945: V-J Day (Victory over Japan Day) in Times Square, New York City.

Celebrations broke out all over America. But then the bells stopped ringing and the cheering subsided. America began to make the transition from wartime to peacetime. Factories converted back to making civilian goods: bicycles, vacuum cleaners, cribs, and cars. Millions of military men returned home to their families and jobs.

Anticipating the end of the war, the WMC had conducted its last propaganda campaign to recruit women war workers in early 1944. In late 1944 the WMC asked the OWI to stop all of its efforts to recruit women. Now the government and industry started producing propaganda to sell women the idea that it was their patriotic duty to return home, to take care of their husbands and children. Stories about women riveters, welders, scientists, and taxicab drivers disappeared from the magazines and newspapers. The OWI's *War Magazine Guide* asked magazine editors to publish stories about jobs for women in the postwar job market. According to the *Guide,* the best jobs for women in postwar America would be found in teaching, nursing, and clerical work, traditionally women's work. Writers for the Writers' War Board published stories about women workers who cheerfully gave up their work tools and lived happily ever after as full-time housewives and mothers.

Some women left voluntarily, but most were laid off. According to Charlcia Neuman, who was a wartime riveter, "I was laid off in September of '45. I just got a slip of paper saying that I wouldn't be needed again. Most of us went at the same time; it was just a matter that there was no more work. . . . The idea was for the women to go back home. The women understood that. And the men had been promised their jobs when they came back." By 1946, over three million women had left the workforce.

Some women did not mind losing their jobs. "I was ready to go home. I was tired," Neuman said later. According to Helen Studer, who had worked as a riveter, "I was glad it was over. I wasn't working 'cause I wanted to. I was working 'cause I thought it was necessary. I thought, I'm going to stay home and be a housewife. My husband never wanted me to work in the first place."

But many women *did* mind losing their jobs. Ottilie Juliet Gattuss, who had worked at Grumman Aircraft Engineering

An article that appeared in the October 31, 1944, edition of Boeing's Trailing Edge News, *a newsletter published during the war for the employees of South Tacoma Branch Plant 684 in Washington.*

"Curtains" for the Axis; Lace Curtains for Her

LORRAINE BLUM, riveter, 684, likes to build Boeing bombers to help knock out the Nips and Nazis.

"But as soon as it's curtains for the Axis, it's going to be lace curtains for me," says

Lorraine Blume

Lorraine. "I want to establish my own home and stay put."

In order to buy that home, she is buying bonds now. When her husband returns from the South Pacific, she hopes to have enough money to get the house she dreams about.

A 1943 cartoon from the Des Moines Register *reflects the fear that after the war, women would not easily give up their new financial independence and strength of spirit.*

Corporation for the duration of the war, wrote a letter to President Truman after she had been laid off. "I happen to be a widow with a mother and son to support. . . . I would like to know why, after serving a company in good faith for almost three and a half years, it is now impossible to obtain employment with them. I am a lathe hand and was classified as skilled labor, but simply because I happen to be a woman I am not wanted."

In Highland Park, Michigan, 200 women who had been laid off at the Ford plant conducted a protest. Marching in front of the plant, the women carried signs that read "Stop Discrimination Because of Sex" "Ford Hires New Help—We Walk the Streets" and "How Come No Work for Women?"

After Nona Pool was laid off as a welder, she tried again and again to get another welding job. She later recalled one of her many unsuccessful experiences. "I said [to the employer], 'Hey, how about giving me a job welding?' and the guy, he turned around and looked at me and kind of laughed. He says, 'Oh,' he says, 'I wouldn't doubt you're a good welder, but we don't have facilities for women.' I said, 'I'll bring my own potty, just bring me a curtain.'"

Jobs were still available for Gattuss and Pool and women like them, but they were mostly jobs like the ones women had had before the war: low-paying, low status, and with not much chance for advancement. According to shipyard worker Nell Conley, "There were very few jobs women could take [after the war] where their salary was anywhere near what a man's would have been for the same kind of work, and there were many, many kinds of work that were simply out of bounds for women."

Edna Hopkins went from welding to "punching a typewriter." Kay Baker went from a shipyard to a grocery store. When Baker realized that many job opportunities for women had ended with the war, she decided that she had "better find a niche." Baker later explained, "I thought there wouldn't be any soldier boys lining up to be grocery clerks, and so that's what I decided to be."

The opening and then the closing of the door to nontraditional job opportunities for women had happened before in America—in particular, every time there was a war. Women did men's jobs

A detail from an etching by Winslow Homer of women filling cartridges at the U.S. Arsenal at Watertown, Massachusetts, during the Civil War. This image appeared on the front cover of Harper's Weekly *on July 20, 1861.*

during the Revolutionary War. During the Civil War, women were hired for the first time as government clerks—at about half the salary of male clerks. Women went to work in factories and arsenals. In Newport, Rhode Island, Katharine Wormeley started a factory to make shirts for the Union army. She hired only wives and other female relatives of soldiers, who had to earn money to support themselves.

During World War I, millions of women were hired to do traditionally male jobs. They were streetcar conductors, business managers, and railroad workers. Women operated machinery, unloaded freight, built dirigibles and gliders, worked in lumber mills and steel mills, and made munitions. After World War I, one official noted that "fifty percent of the number of employees in our explosive plants were women who braved the dangers connected with this line of work and to which they had been entirely unaccustomed."

But during World War II, the mobilization of women workers was extraordinary. Never before had the government and industry launched nationwide propaganda campaigns to recruit women workers. Never before had so many women responded. And although three million women left the workforce by 1946, there were still more women in the workforce than there had been before the war began. By 1948, despite their limited job opportunities, the number of women in the workforce started to increase again and record numbers of women continued to enter the workforce in the 1990s. Unfortunately, many of the problems working women faced in World War II still

Women workers during World War I.

Chippers in a shipyard in Sausalito, California, burn imperfections off the metal surface.

exist, including inequality in wages, shortage of affordable child care, hostility and harassment from male workers, and the demands of keeping house, caring for a family, and having a career. In addition, many jobs that were open to women during World War II are still filled mostly by men.

As they lived their lives after World War II, many women war workers did not talk about their experience. For some women it was too painful to remember how quickly their careers as welders, riveters, and crane operators had ended. Other women who were working hard just to survive did not have time to reminisce. Many women felt that people were not interested in their stories, especially during the 1950s, when there was an escalating trend toward blaming working women for problems ranging from juvenile delinquency to divorce.

But women war workers never forgot the job experience that they had for the duration of World War II. They never forgot the thrill of getting a chance to do a war job and doing it. They never forgot the satisfaction of earning good wages. They never forgot the excitement of being independent. They never forgot that once there was a time in America when women were told that they could do anything.

And they did.

Welders working at Morin Shipyard in Sausalito, California. Note in the background the welder's name, Mary, and her identification number written on her hood.

SELECT LIST OF WOMEN'S WARTIME JOBS

Many magazine articles were written about women war workers during World War II. These articles always included examples of jobs that women were doing.

"The Margin Now Is Womanpower," *Fortune* magazine, February 1943:
Barber, butcher, taxi driver, railroad track tender, forest fire fighter, whistle punk in logging camp, aerodynamic engineer, keel welder, riveter, ticket taker, mechanic, cargo loader, and checker for commercial airlines.

"Women in Steel," *Life* magazine, August 9, 1943:
Flame cutter, metallurgical observer, laborer, welder, blacksmith's helper, flame burner, core maker, scraper, scarfer, pan man, crane operator, tool machinist, electrical helper, grinder, oiler, coil taper, foundry helper, checker, loader, cleaning and maintenance worker, inspector, draw-bench operator, engine operator, furnace operator, billet operation helper, packer and shipper.

"Women at Work," *National Geographic* magazine, August 1944:
Flash welder, shipfitter, chipper, physicist, driver, supervisor, tinsmith, pipe fitter, chemist, surveyor, attorney, messenger, scaler, draftsman, consultant, ordnance worker, astronomer, motorman, mathematician, bus driver, milkman, postman, fireman, street cleaner, traffic cop, lumberjack, telegraph operator, steam hammer operator, radio engineer, electrical engineer, geologist, meteorologist, shell assembler, architect, flagpole painter, junk sorter, garbage collector, scientist, conductor, baggageman, drawbridge tender, crossing flagman, electrician, and brain picker, stomach scrubber, belly grader, sweetbread puller, and vein pumper in slaughterhouses.

FACTS & FIGURES ABOUT WOMEN WAR WORKERS

1. Between 1940 and 1944, the number of employed women increased from 12 million to 18.2 million. In 1947, two years after World War II ended, the number of employed women was 15.8 million, a higher number than in 1940 but lower than in 1944.

2. Of all women age 14 and up, 27.4 percent were in the labor force in 1940, compared to 35 percent in 1944 and 29.8 percent in 1947.

3. Before World War II, women in the labor force were generally young and single. By the end of the war, women in the labor force were generally married and over 35 years old.

4. Of the women who entered the labor force for the first time during the war, 60 percent were over the age of 35, 17.3 percent were between the ages of 14 and 19, 22.2 percent were between the ages of 20 and 24, and one-half of one percent were between the ages of 25 and 34.

5. During World War II, the number of wives working doubled.

6. Wives of servicemen who were away from home were three times as likely to work as wives whose husbands were not away from home.

7. Of the women who worked during World War II, two million were clerical workers and one million worked for the federal government.

8. During World War II, the number of women journalists in Washington, D.C., jumped from 30 to 98.

9. During World War II, corporate profits increased from $6.4 billion to $10.8 billion.

10. Of the women who were working in March 1944, 2,690,000 were employed as factory workers. Of the women factory workers, 49 percent of them had not been in the labor force before the war, 31 percent had been housewives, 16 percent had been students, and 2 percent had been involved in other activities.

11. In Detroit, Michigan, 44,064 women were employed in manufacturing in 1940 compared to: 71,000 in 1942, 269,000 in November 1943, 124,000

after V-E Day in 1945, 66,900 after V-J Day in 1945, 63,300 in February 1946.

12. Because of a shortage of waitresses, one-third of the restaurants in Detroit were closed by late 1943.

13. During World War II, the number of black women who were poorly paid domestic workers declined from 72 percent to 40 percent. The proportion of black women who were better-paid factory workers increased from 7.3 percent to 18.6 percent.

14. In April 1941, the proportion of women in the aircraft industry (excluding aircraft-engine manufacturing) was 1 percent, compared to 39 percent in June 1943.

15. By the end of 1942, 11,300 women were working in three Kaiser shipyards in Oregon: 34 percent held traditionally female jobs, while 66 percent held traditionally male jobs.

16. In 1943, over three million women belonged to labor unions, compared to 800,000 in 1939. Despite the increase in female membership, men continued to hold most of the significant positions at both the local and national level.

17. The widely read weekly magazine, the *Saturday Evening Post,* had 20 stories in 1943 that featured women doing war work, compared to no stories in 1941 and one story in 1946.

18. In a survey, 81 percent of the women employed at the Springfield Arsenal in Springfield, Massachusetts, said they hoped to continue working after the war. But within one week of V-J Day, every woman had been fired.

19. In Detroit, a survey found that 72 percent of women workers who had been laid off after the war wanted to work, but they couldn't find any jobs.

20. A year after World War II ended, three and a half million women had voluntarily—or involuntarily—left the labor force.

CHRONOLOGY

1939
September 1
Germany invades Poland and
World War II begins.

1940
January 3
FDR calls for an increased
production of planes.

October 29
First peacetime military draft in
the U.S. begins.

December 20
FDR creates the Office of
Production Management,
predecessor to the War
Production Board (WPB).

1941
January
FDR proclaims the United States
the "Arsenal of Democracy."

June
FDR signs Executive Order 8802
banning discrimination because
of race or religion in hiring
people for defense and
government jobs.

June 22
Germany invades USSR.

November
Advertisers form the War
Advertising Council.

December 7
Japanese attack Pearl Harbor.

December 8
United States declares war on
Japan.

December 11
Germany and Italy declare war
on United States.

1942
January
FDR calls for production of
60,000 planes, 45,000 tanks, and
20,000 antiaircraft guns.

January 16
FDR creates War Production
Board (WPB).

January 28
FDR creates Office of Civilian
Defense (OCD).

April
FDR creates War Manpower
Commission (WMC).

May
Sugar is rationed.
June 3–6
United States wins Battle of
Midway.

June 13
FDR creates Office of War
Information (OWI).

August 7
U.S. troops land on Guadalcanal.

September
Nationwide rationing of gasoline
begins.

1943
September
"Women in Necessary Service"
campaign launched by WMC
and OWI.
Italy surrenders.

1944
Spring
"Women in War" campaign conducted by WMC, OWI, and U.S. War Department.

May 3
Meat rationing begins.

June 6
D-day.

July 21
U.S. troops land on Guam.

August 4
The WPB decides to allow the production of various domestic appliances such as stoves and vacuum cleaners.

Winter
WMC asks the OWI to end its campaign to recruit women war workers.

December 16
Battle of the Bulge.

1945
February 19
U.S. Marines land on Iwo Jima.

April 12
FDR dies and Harry Truman becomes president.

April 30
Hitler commits suicide.

May 7
German troops surrender unconditionally.

May 8
V-E (Victory in Europe) Day celebrated.

August 6
Atomic bomb dropped on Hiroshima.

August 9
Atomic bomb dropped on Nagasaki.

August 14
Japan surrenders unconditionally and World War II ends. The war directly involved 57 nations and an estimated 54.8 million people, mostly civilians, died. V-J (Victory over Japan) Day is celebrated.

August 19
Gasoline and fuel rationing ends.

September 2
Japan and Allies sign official surrender agreement.

October 30
Nationwide shoe rationing ends.

November 23
Food rationing on all items except sugar ends.

December 30
Nationwide rationing of tires ends.

BIBLIOGRAPHY AND NOTES

Books

Anderson, Karen. *Wartime Women: Sex Roles, Family Relations, and Status During World War II.* Westport, CT: Greenwood Press, 1981.

Bailey, Ronald H., and the Editors of Time-Life Books. *World War II: The Home Front: USA.* Alexandria, VA: Time-Life Books, 1978.

Baker, Laura. *Wanted—Women in War Industry: The Complete Guide to a War Factory Job.* New York: E. P. Dutton, 1943.

Baxandall, Rosalyn, Linda Gordon, and Susan Reverby. *America's Working Women: A Documentary History 1600 to the Present.* New York: Vintage Books, 1976.

Boardman, Barrington. *Flappers, Bootleggers, "Typhoid Mary," and the Bomb: An Anecdotal History of the United States from 1923–1945.* New York: Harper & Row Publishers, 1988.

Campbell, D'Ann. *Women at War with America: Private Lives in a Patriotic Era.* Cambridge, MA: Harvard University Press, 1985.

Casdorph, Paul D. *Let the Good Times Roll: Life at Home in America during WW II.* New York: Paragon House, 1989.

Chafe, William H. *The American Woman: Her Changing Social, Economic, and Political Roles, 1920–1970.* New York: Oxford University Press, 1972.

Chafe, William H. *The Unfinished Journey: America Since World War II, 2nd Ed.* New York: Oxford University Press, 1991.

Churchill, Jan. *On Wings to War: Teresa James, Aviator.* Manhattan, KS: Sunflower University Press, 1992.

Cohen, Stan. *V for Victory: America's Home Front During World War II.* Missoula, MT: Pictorial Histories Publishing Company, Inc., 1991.

Dickson, Paul. *Timelines: Day by Day and Trend by Trend from the Dawn of the Atomic Age to the Close of the Cold War.* Reading, MA: Addison-Wesley Publishing Company, Inc., 1990.

Evans, Sara M. *Born for Liberty: A History of Women in America.* New York: The Free Press, 1989.

Frank, Miriam, Marilyn Ziebarth, and Connie Field. *The Life and Times of Rosie the Riveter: The Story of Three Million Working Women During World War II.* Emeryville, CA: Clarity Educational Productions, 1982.

Freeman, Joshua et al. *Who Built America?, Vol 2.* New York: Pantheon Books, 1992.

Fussell, Paul. *Wartime: Understanding and Behavior in the Second World War.* New York: Oxford University Press, 1988.

Giddings, Paula. *When and Where I Enter: The Impact of Black Women on Race and Sex in America*. New York: Bantam Books, 1984.

Giles, Nell. *Punch in, Susie!* New York: Harper and Brothers, 1943.

Gluck, Sherna Berger. *Rosie the Riveter Revisited: Women, the War, and Social Change*. Boston: Twayne Publishers, 1987.

Good Work, Sister! Study Guide Portland, OR: Northwest Women's History Project, 1982.

Harris, Mark Jonathan, Franklin D. Mitchell, and Steven J. Schechter. *The Homefront: America During World War II*. New York: G. P. Putnam's Sons, 1984.

Hartmann, Susan M. *The Home Front and Beyond: American Women in the 1940s*. Boston: Twayne Publishers, 1982.

Hoehling, A. A. *Home Front, U.S.A.: The Story of World War II Over Here*. New York: Thomas Y. Crowell Company, 1966.

Honey, Maureen. *Creating Rosie the Riveter: Class, Gender, and Propaganda During World War II*. Amherst: University of Massachusetts Press, 1984.

Hoopes, Roy. *Americans Remember the Home Front*. New York: Hawthorn Books, Inc., 1977.

Jaffe, Walter. *The Last Liberty: The Biography of the S.S. Jeremiah O'Brien*. Palo Alto, CA: Glencannon Press, 1993.

Jones, Jacqueline. *Labor of Love, Labor of Sorrow: Black Women, Work, and the Family from Slavery to the Present*. New York: Basic Books, 1985.

Keegan, John. *The Second World War*. New York: Viking, 1990.

Keil, Sally Van Wagenen. *Those Wonderful Women in Their Flying Machines: The Unknown Heroines of World War II*. New York: Rawson, Wade Publishers, Inc., 1979.

Kessler-Harris, Alice. *Out to Work: A History of Wage-Earning Women in the United States*. New York: Oxford University Press, 1982.

Lawson, Don. *An Album of World War II Home Fronts*. New York: Franklin Watts, 1980.

Litoff, Judy Barrett et al. *Miss You: The World War II Letters of Barbara Wooddall Taylor and Charles E. Taylor*. Athens: The University of Georgia Press, 1990.

Lockwood, Allison McCrillis. *Touched with Fire: An American Community in World War II*. Northampton, MA: Daily Hampshire Gazette, 1993.

Macy, Sue. *A Whole New Ball Game: The Story of the All-American Girls' Professional Baseball League*. New York: Henry Holt and Company, Inc., 1993.

May, Elaine Tyler. *Pushing the Limits: American Women 1940–1961*. New York: Oxford University Press, 1994.

Miklos, Josephine von. *I Took a War Job*. New York: Simon and Schuster, 1943.

Milkman, Ruth. *Gender at Work: The Dynamics of Job Segregation by Sex During World War II*. Urbana: University of Illinois Press, 1987.

Perrett, Geoffrey. *Days of Sadness, Years of Triumph: The American People, 1939–1945*. New York: Coward, McCann & Geoghegan, Inc., 1973.

Riley, Glenda. *Inventing the American Woman: A Perspective on Women's History, 1965 to the Present, Vol. II*. Arlington Heights, IL: Harlan Davidson, Inc., 1986.

Rosenberg, Rosalind. *Divided Lives: American Women in the Twentieth Century*. New York: Hill and Wang, 1992.

Ruiz, Vicki L. *Cannery Women, Cannery Lives: Mexican Women, Unionization, and the*

California Food-Processing Industry, 1930–1950. Albuquerque: University of New Mexico Press, 1987.

Rupp, Leila. *Mobilizing Women for War: German and American Propaganda, 1939–1945*. Princeton, NJ: Princeton University Press, 1978.

Terkel, Studs. *"The Good War": An Oral History of World War Two*. New York: Pantheon Books, 1984.

The War in Women's Employment: The Experience of the United Kingdom and the United States. Montreal: International Labour Office, 1946.

Weatherford, Doris. *American Women and World War II*. New York: Facts on File, Inc., 1990.

Winkler, Allan M. *Home Front U.S.A.: America During World War II*. Arlington Heights, IL: Harlan Davidson, Inc., 1986.

Winkler, Allan M. *The Politics of Propaganda: The Office of War Information 1942-1945*. New Haven, CT: Yale University Press, 1978.

Women in Industry. World War II Documents from the National Archives. Dubuque, IA: Kendall/Hunt Publishing Company.

Articles

Adams, Frank S. "Women in Democracy's Arsenal." *The New York Times Magazine* (October 19, 1941): 10.

Anderson, Karen. "Last Hired, First Fired: Black Women Workers During World War II." *Journal of American History* 69 (June 1982): 82–97.

Bourke-White, Margaret. "Women in Steel." *Life* (August 9, 1943): 74–81.

Bradley, La Verne. "Women at Work." *National Geographic* (August 1944): 193–220

"'Curtains' for the Axis; Lace Curtains for Her." *Boeing News Tacoma Edition* (October 31, 1944): 3.

"Draft for Women." *Business Week* (July 11, 1942): 72.

"Girl Pilots." *Life* (July 19, 1943): 7–9.

"How War Drive Hits Home Front." *Business Week* (March 10, 1945): 15–16.

"Industry Deaths Since Pearl Harbor 37,600, Exceeding by 7,500 Number Killed in War." *New York Times* (January 21, 1944): 34.

"Ladies of Washington's Working Press." *Newsweek* (March 1, 1943): 64.

"The Margin Now Is Womanpower." *Fortune* (February 1943): 99–102, 222–224.

Meyer, Elisabeth. "'Ma's Making Bombers!'" *Reader's Digest* (October 1942): 49–53.

Mezerik, A. G. "Getting Rid of the Women." *Atlantic Monthly* 175 (June 1945): 79–83.

"Mrs. Herrick Discusses Training of Women for Jobs in Shipyards." *New York Times* (September 1, 1942): 15.

"Nation Appraises Its Womanpower." *Business Week* (May 16, 1942): 22.

"190,000 Workers." *Business Week* (September 5, 1942): 33–34, 36.

Quick, Paddy. "Rosie the Riveter: Myths and Realities." *Radical America* 9 (July-August 1945): 33–36.

"Seattle—A Boom Comes Back." *Business Week* (June 20, 1942): 26–32.

Stolz, Lois Meek. "The Nursery Comes to the Shipyard." *The New York Times Magazine* (November 7, 1943): 20, 39.

"Symphony Goes Co-Ed." *Newsweek* (December 6, 1943): 86.

"3,500 Women Apply for Shipyard Jobs." *New York Times* (October 4, 1944): 43.

Tobias, Sheila, and Lisa Anderson. "Whatever Really Happened to Rosie the Riveter? Demobilization and the Female Labor Force, 1944–1947." MSS Modular Publications, Inc. New York, *Module 9* (1974): 1–36.

"Tremendous Skilled Labor Pool Faces Demobilization Planners." *Newsweek* (August 23, 1943): 51–57.

"26 Women Get Jobs at Todd Shipyards." *New York Times* (October 6, 1942): 20.

"Welder Launches Tank-Landing Ship." *New York Times* (December 14, 1942): 28.

"Where Shortages Pinch Consumer." *Business Week* (April 4, 1942): 9.

"Woman's Place." *Business Week* (May 16, 1942): 20, 22.

"Women at Work." *Newsweek* (January 5, 1942): 36.

"Women for War." *Business Week* (August 15, 1942): 24.

"Women in Democracy's Arsenal." *The New York Times Magazine* (October 10, 1941): 10, 29.

"Women—Now!" *Business Week* (January 9, 1943): 98.

"Women's Factory." *Business Week* (July 4, 1942): 20–21.

Videos and Films

Field, Connie (Producer and Director). *The Life and Times of Rosie the Riveter*. Emeryville, CA: Clarity Educational Productions, 1982.

Good Work, Sister! Portland OR: Northwest Women's History Project, 1982.

Women in Defense. Davenport, IA: Blackhawk Films, 1941.

Women In American Life, 1942–1955: War Work, Housework, and Growing Discontent. Windsor, CA: National Women's History Project, 1988.

Notes

The quotations from Dot Chastney Emer are taken from taped interviews with the author. Quotations by women war workers are primarily drawn from the following oral histories: The Northwest Women's History Project's *Good Work, Sister!*; Sherna Berger Gluck's *Rosie the Riveter Revisited: Women, the War, and Social Change; The Homefront: America During World War II* by Mark Jonathan Harris, et al.; and Studs Terkel's *"The Good War": An Oral History of World War II*. Information about the Office of War Information's propaganda campaign and women war workers was largely drawn from Maureen Honey's *Creating Rosie the Riveter: Class, Gender, and Propaganda During World War II*; Karen Anderson's *Wartime Women: Sex Roles, Family Relations, and Status During World War II*; and Leila Rupp's *Mobilizing Women for War: German and American Propaganda, 1939–1945*. Statistics were primarily drawn from D'Ann Campbell's *Women at War with America: Private Lives in a Patriotic Era*; William Chafe's *The American Woman: Her Changing Social, Economic, and Political Roles, 1920–1970*; and Sheila Tobias and Lisa Anderson's "Whatever Really Happened to Rosie the Riveter." Specific information about magazine and newspaper articles cited in the text can be found in the bibliography.

PICTURE CREDITS

ACKNOWLEDGMENTS

First and foremost, I extend my gratitude to all of the women who were pioneers in the workplace during World War II and who either talked with me or created an oral history that I read. I am also grateful to all of the people who talked with me about their experience on the home front, especially Dorothy Chastney Emer. In addition, thanks to Kay Althoff, Hedy Leutner, Terry Gianzinetti, Jackie Brock Magness, Lila Kuhn, Sarah Goldstein, Dorothy Compton, and George and Mary Hickson. Thanks to the Northwest Women's History Project for permission to use material from *Good Work, Sister!*

In the course of my research, I received assistance from many wonderful and informative people to whom I am grateful, including Molly Murphy MacGregor and Susanne Otteman, National Women's History Project, Windsor, California; Pat Jollota, Archivist, and Gus Norwood, Director, Clark County Historical Museum, Vancouver, Washington; Tom Lubbesmeyer, Archival Specialist, and Marilyn A. Phipps, Archivist Historian, The Boeing Company, Seattle, Washington; Barbara Gundle, Northwest Women's History Project, Portland, Oregon; Miriam Frank, New York University, New York; Emily Rosenberg, Macalester College, St. Paul, Minnesota; and Mary Woodward, National Liberty Ship Memorial, SS *Jeremiah O'Brien*, San Francisco, California. Other people were helpful in providing illustrations and photographs, including Tom

Rockwell, Stephen Colman, Stan Cohen, Pip Stromgren, Mark Renovitch, Shirley Nieman, Jocelyn Clapp, Barbara Conover, Greg Cheadle, Mary Yearwood, Josh Brown, Jan Berenstain, Lynne Rohmerien, Carol Pickerl, and Brian Haviland.

In my quest to uncover the actual origin of "Rosie the Riveter," I was fortunate to talk with a variety of people who had different pieces of the puzzle, including Charles A. Ruch, Archivist and Historian, Westinghouse Electric Corporation, Pittsburgh, Pennsylvania, who was at Westinghouse when J. Howard Miller created the "We Can Do It" poster; Lois Lovisolo, Historian, Grumman Corporation, Bethpage, New York, who interviewed Rose Bonavita; Janet Loeb, widow of John Jacob Loeb, who wrote the music for the song, "Rosie the Riveter"; Charles Silver, Curator, Museum of Modern Art Film Study Center, New York City; Robert Lissauer, New York City, author of *Lissauer's Encyclopedia of Popular Music in America,* and former colleague of Redd Evans, who wrote the lyrics for the song and John Jacob Loeb; Mary Doyle Keefe, the model for Norman Rockwell's *Saturday Evening Post* cover "Rosie"; Maureen Hart Hennessy, Marshall Stoltz, and Dorothy Grant, who provided information about Norman Rockwell and his painting; Geraldine Hoff Doyle, whose photograph may have been used by J. Howard Miller; Geraldine Doyle's sister M. Virginia Hoff Watson; Tom Fortunato, Sales Operation Manager and Program Coordinator, National Archives Museum Shop, Washington, D.C.; and Archie Green, a former World War II welder and folklore historian from San Francisco who knew about Wendy the Welder.

In writing this book, I have had the pleasure of working with an enthusiastic, dedicated, and determined editor, Jill Davis, who approached me about this book after seeing Connie Field's *The Life and Times of Rosie the Riveter.* And as always, I had the unwavering good cheer and support of my friends and family, including those who read parts or all of the various versions of my manuscript and offered candid and useful comments. To them—Linda Hickson, Margot Zahner, Ann Sparanese, Bob Guild, Dana Bilsky, Jonathan Colman, David Colman, and Stephen Colman—I offer my heartfelt and eternal gratitude.

Index

Page numbers in **boldface** refer to illustrations.